CONTENTS

LEGISLATION TO REDUCE MEDICAL ERRORS

HEARING

BEFORE THE

SUBCOMMITTEE ON HEALTH

OF THE

COMMITTEE ON WAYS AND MEANS
HOUSE OF REPRESENTATIVES

ONE HUNDRED SEVENTH CONGRESS

SECOND SESSION

SEPTEMBER 10, 2002

Serial No. 107–95

Printed for the use of the Committee on Ways and Means

U.S. GOVERNMENT PRINTING OFFICE

86–199 WASHINGTON : 2003

For sale by the Superintendent of Documents, U.S. Government Printing Office
Internet: bookstore.gpo.gov Phone: toll free (866) 512–1800; DC area (202) 512–1800
Fax: (202) 512–2250 Mail: Stop SSOP, Washington, DC 20402–0001

COMMITTEE ON WAYS AND MEANS

BILL THOMAS, California, *Chairman*

PHILIP M. CRANE, Illinois
E. CLAY SHAW, Jr., Florida
NANCY L. JOHNSON, Connecticut
AMO HOUGHTON, New York
WALLY HERGER, California
JIM MCCRERY, Louisiana
DAVE CAMP, Michigan
JIM RAMSTAD, Minnesota
JIM NUSSLE, Iowa
SAM JOHNSON, Texas
JENNIFER DUNN, Washington
MAC COLLINS, Georgia
ROB PORTMAN, Ohio
PHIL ENGLISH, Pennsylvania
WES WATKINS, Oklahoma
J.D. HAYWORTH, Arizona
JERRY WELLER, Illinois
KENNY C. HULSHOF, Missouri
SCOTT MCINNIS, Colorado
RON LEWIS, Kentucky
MARK FOLEY, Florida
KEVIN BRADY, Texas
PAUL RYAN, Wisconsin

CHARLES B. RANGEL, New York
FORTNEY PETE STARK, California
ROBERT T. MATSUI, California
WILLIAM J. COYNE, Pennsylvania
SANDER M. LEVIN, Michigan
BENJAMIN L. CARDIN, Maryland
JIM MCDERMOTT, Washington
GERALD D. KLECZKA, Wisconsin
JOHN LEWIS, Georgia
RICHARD E. NEAL, Massachusetts
MICHAEL R. MCNULTY, New York
WILLIAM J. JEFFERSON, Louisiana
JOHN S. TANNER, Tennessee
XAVIER BECERRA, California
KAREN L. THURMAN, Florida
LLOYD DOGGETT, Texas
EARL POMEROY, North Dakota

Allison Giles, *Chief of Staff*
Janice Mays, *Minority Chief Counsel*

SUBCOMMITTEE ON HEALTH

NANCY L. JOHNSON, Connecticut, *Chairman*

JIM MCCRERY, Louisiana
PHILIP M. CRANE, Illinois
SAM JOHNSON, Texas
DAVE CAMP, Michigan
JIM RAMSTAD, Minnesota
PHIL ENGLISH, Pennsylvania
JENNIFER DUNN, Washington

FORTNEY PETE STARK, California
GERALD D. KLECZKA, Wisconsin
JOHN LEWIS, Georgia
JIM MCDERMOTT, Washington
KAREN L. THURMAN, Florida

Pursuant to clause 2(e)(4) of Rule XI of the Rules of the House, public hearing records of the Committee on Ways and Means are also published in electronic form. **The printed hearing record remains the official version.** Because electronic submissions are used to prepare both printed and electronic versions of the hearing record, the process of converting between various electronic formats may introduce unintentional errors or omissions. Such occurrences are inherent in the current publication process and should diminish as the process is further refined.

LEGISLATION TO REDUCE MEDICAL ERRORS

TUESDAY, SEPTEMBER 10, 2002

HOUSE OF REPRESENTATIVES,
COMMITTEE ON WAYS AND MEANS,
SUBCOMMITTEE ON HEALTH,
Washington, DC.

The Subcommittee met, pursuant to notice, at 11:48 a.m., in room B–318, Rayburn House Office Building, Hon. Nancy L. Johnson (Chairman of the Subcommittee) presiding.

[The advisory and the revised advisory announcing the hearing follow:]

ADVISORY

FROM THE COMMITTEE ON WAYS AND MEANS

SUBCOMMITTEE ON HEALTH

FOR IMMEDIATE RELEASE
September 3, 2002
No. HL–17

CONTACT: (202) 225–3943

Johnson Announces Hearing on Legislation to Reduce Medical Errors

Congresswoman Nancy L. Johnson (R–CT), Chairman, Subcommittee on Health of the Committee on Ways and Means, today announced that the Subcommittee will hold a hearing on legislation to reduce medical errors. **The hearing will take place on Tuesday, September 10, 2002, in the main Committee hearing room, 1100 Longworth House Office Building, beginning at 10:00 a.m.**

In view of the limited time available to hear witnesses, oral testimony at this hearing will be from invited witnesses only. Witnesses will include academic experts and representatives from professional organizations. However, any individual or organization not scheduled for an oral appearance may submit a written statement for consideration by the Committee and for inclusion in the printed record of the hearing.

BACKGROUND:

H.R. 4889, the "Patient Safety Improvement Act of 2002," was introduced by Chairman Johnson on June 6, 2002. The bill seeks to reduce medical errors by encouraging reporting of adverse events to new patient safety organizations. These new organizations would analyze what went wrong and provide feedback to health providers so that they can learn from their mistakes. This hearing builds on the testimony provided at the Subcommittee's March 7, 2002, hearing on medical errors.

Medical errors permeate our health system. More than three years ago, the Institute of Medicine (IOM) reported that preventable medical errors are the eighth leading cause of death in America—ahead of breast cancer, AIDS and traffic deaths. Nearly 100,000 patients die in hospitals each year as a result of preventable mistakes. The number of injured is even greater. And yet in the three years since the release of the breakthrough IOM report, no legislation has passed either chamber of Congress.

In announcing the hearing, Chairman Johnson stated, "We have spent too much time discussing the potential for quality improvement and fewer errors in health care. It is clear that Federal leadership can make a difference and Congress can make that happen. I am looking forward to thoughtful input and a lively discussion to help us in our consideration of this bill."

FOCUS OF THE HEARING:

Tuesday's hearing will focus on the draft Chairman's mark of H.R. 4889.

DETAILS FOR SUBMISSION OF WRITTEN COMMENTS:

Please Note: Due to the change in House mail policy, any person or organization wishing to submit a written statement for the printed record of the hearing should send it electronically to hearingclerks.waysandmeans@mail.house.gov, along with a fax copy to (202) 225–2610, by the close of business, Thursday, September 12, 2002.

Those filing written statements who wish to have their statements distributed to the press and interested public at the hearing should deliver their 200 copies to the Subcommittee on Health in room 1136 Longworth House Office Building, in an open and searchable package 48 hours before the hearing. The U.S. Capitol Police will refuse sealed-packaged deliveries to all House Office Buildings.

FORMATTING REQUIREMENTS:

Each statement presented for printing to the Committee by a witness, any written statement or exhibit submitted for the printed record or any written comments in response to a request for written comments must conform to the guidelines listed below. Any statement or exhibit not in compliance with these guidelines will not be printed, but will be maintained in the Committee files for review and use by the Committee.

1. Due to the change in House mail policy, all statements and any accompanying exhibits for printing must be submitted electronically to hearingclerks.waysandmeans@mail.house.gov, along with a fax copy to (202) 225–2610, in Word Perfect or MS Word format and MUST NOT exceed a total of 10 pages including attachments. Witnesses are advised that the Committee will rely on electronic submissions for printing the official hearing record.

2. Copies of whole documents submitted as exhibit material will not be accepted for printing. Instead, exhibit material should be referenced and quoted or paraphrased. All exhibit material not meeting these specifications will be maintained in the Committee files for review and use by the Committee.

3. Any statements must include a list of all clients, persons, or organizations on whose behalf the witness appears. A supplemental sheet must accompany each statement listing the name, company, address, telephone and fax numbers of each witness.

Note: All Committee advisories and news releases are available on the World Wide Web at http://waysandmeans.house.gov.

The Committee seeks to make its facilities accessible to persons with disabilities. If you are in need of special accommodations, please call (202) 225–1721 or (202) 226–3411 TTD/TTY in advance of the event (four business days notice is requested). Questions with regard to special accommodation needs in general (including availability of Committee materials in alternative formats) may be directed to the Committee as noted above.

*** * * NOTICE—CHANGE IN TIME * * ***

ADVISORY

FROM THE COMMITTEE ON WAYS AND MEANS

SUBCOMMITTEE ON HEALTH

FOR IMMEDIATE RELEASE
September 6, 2002
No. HL–17–Revised

CONTACT: (202) 225–3943

Johnson Announces Hearing on Change in Time for Subcommittee Hearing on Legislation to Reduce Medical Errors

Congresswoman Nancy L. Johnson (R–CT), Chairman, Subcommittee on Health of the Committee on Ways and Means, today announced that the Subcommittee hearing on legislation to reduce medical errors, scheduled for Tuesday, September 10, 2002, at 10:00 a.m., in the main Committee hearing room, 1100 Longworth House Office Building, **will now be held at 11:00 a.m.**

All other details for the hearing remain the same. (See Subcommittee Advisory No. HL–17, dated September 3, 2002.)

Chairman JOHNSON. The Committee will come to order. Mr. Stark is on his way back from the Floor and I thought I would get us moving. My apologies, Mr. Secretary, for the long delay. These things are beyond our control.

I want to remind the Committee that it was more than 3 years ago that the Institute of Medicine (IOM) reported that preventable medical errors are the eighth leading cause of death in America. These are ahead of breast cancer, AIDS, and traffic deaths. Yet no legislation has been approved by any Committee in either chamber of Congress to deal with this crisis. Nearly 100,000 patients die in hospitals each year as a result of preventable mistakes, and the number of injured is far greater. Clearly, it is time to act.

The draft Chairman's mark, which is before the Committee at this time, extends confidentiality protection and privilege standards to patient safety data that is reported externally to new Patient Safety Organizations (PSO). These certified and independent organizations will analyze the reports from health care providers and provide feedback on what went wrong and how to fix it. Reporting adverse events and close calls allows us to gain insight into how to prevent errors. By protecting reporters, we will stimulate a rich process that should enable providers to dramatically improve the quality of health care.

The bill also establishes a new Center for Patient Safety within U.S. Department of Health and Human Services (HHS) to be the focal point of Administration policy on patient safety. This center will administer a new medical errors database of non-identifiable information. Researchers will use this database to identify national trends and encourage best practices to prevent errors and improve health care quality.

Finally, the bill establishes a process through which new voluntary standards for interoperability can be developed. In our quest for improved health care quality, the urgency for investing in health care information technology is exceeded only by that for investment in patient safety systems. The health care industry has lagged far behind other sectors of our economy in adopting the information systems that can assure continuous quality improvement.

Consequently, we must not only shield the reporting of health care delivery problems from legal liability. We must also support the development of the infrastructure needed to gather data, analyze data, problem solve, and disseminate recommendations for quality improvement. Therefore, the bill establishes a new Technology Advisory Board to provide expert advice to the Secretary in creating interoperability standards. We simply cannot afford to establish broad information systems that do not talk to each other. Patient safety is too important.

That is what H.R. 4889 is designed to do. H.R. 4889 would facilitate the identification of health care delivery problems through voluntary and confidential reporting. It supports the analysis of data and development of recommended best practices. The bill also provides for the dissemination of recommendations for best practices back to the health care industry. All of these activities would be privileged or shielded from discovery for litigation purposes. Fear of legal liability has had a chilling effect on the development of reporting and analysis of errors data that can save lives and create a health care delivery system capable of continuous quality improvement.

This legislation incorporates the recommendations of experts, consumers, policy makers, and my colleagues in Congress. The overwhelming and positive response to our proposal is a testament to the broad recognition in the industry that much more can be done. I am pleased that 50 provider, patient, quality improvement, and national accreditation organizations have endorsed this draft proposal.

Secretary Thompson, you need no introduction to this Committee. I am very pleased that you have worked closely with us, as has Centers for Medicare and Medicaid Services (CMS), the Agency for Healthcare Research Quality (AHRQ), and the U.S. Department of the Treasury and the White House, in developing this draft. I am also very pleased that your testimony will review the great variety of initiatives that you have led to achieve these very same goals of improved patient safety and improved health care quality.

Our second panel is also impressive. Dr. Lucian Leape from Harvard University is a member of the IOM's Committee on Quality of Health Care in America and one of the authors of the 1999 report on errors.

Dr. Michael Wood is President and Chief Executive Officer of the Mayo Foundation and is testifying on behalf of the Health Leadership Council. Also joining us is Ken Segel, Director of the Pittsburgh Regional Healthcare Initiative, whose organization testified at our initial hearing. Dr. Herbert Pardes is the President and

Chief Executive Officer of the New York-Presbyterian Health Care System. He brings a wealth of expertise on information technology and computerized medical records. Jill Rosenthal is a project manager at the National Academy for State Health Policy who will give us a perspective from the State's point of view and experience.

[The opening statement of Chairman Johnson follows:]

Opening Statement of the Hon. Nancy L. Johnson, a Representative in Congress from the State of Connecticut, and Chairman, Subcommittee on Health

More than three years ago, the Institute of Medicine (IOM) reported that preventable medical errors are the eighth leading cause of death in America—ahead of breast cancer, AIDS, and traffic deaths. And yet, no legislation has been approved by any committee or either chamber of Congress to deal with this crisis. Nearly 100,000 patients die in hospitals each year as a result of preventable mistakes. The number of injured is far greater.

Just yesterday, newspapers reported on findings by researchers at Auburn University who analyzed data from 36 hospitals and nursing homes in Colorado and Georgia of an 81-day period in 1999. These researchers found medication errors in about 20% of the doses administered in a "typical" 300-bed facility, and found 7% of the errors "potentially harmful." Not only do medical errors harm and take the lives of innocent, often basically healthy patients, they are costly.

According to the Pittsburgh Healthcare Initiative, medication errors result in $3,500 to $4,000 additional costs per incident, an unacceptable financial cost borne by hospitals, individuals, public health programs and, yes, Medicare.

The evidence of the human and economic costs of errors is simply overwhelming! It's simply time we must act. On March 7 of this year, the Subcommittee held a hearing on this issue, with testimony from some of the country's most highly recognized experts on reducing medical errors. At that hearing, Mr. Stark stated that he hoped our next meeting on this would be a markup. And while we began work immediately, fear developed that any product developed could be used to make the prescription drug bill "bipartisan." Despite assurances, that concern lingered and we laid aside our work on this topic until the prescription drug bill passed the House. Since that time I introduced a base bill on June 6 that was developed with experts' and Member input and then continued to explore aspects of this issue with my colleagues Mrs. Thurman, and Messrs. Houghton, Cardin and Stark that resulted in a new draft Chairman's mark in July.

On August 2, I solicited comments from all members of the IOM Committee that produced the medical errors report. I am pleased that we received near-unanimous support for this new proposal, as well as suggestions for refinements and changes. From this hearing we will propose a final draft for consideration by the full Committee in the near future.

The draft Chairman's mark extends confidentiality protection and privilege standards to patient safety data that are reported externally to new Patient Safety Organizations. These certified and independent organizations will analyze the reports from health care providers and provide feedback on what went wrong and how to fix it. Reporting adverse events and close calls allows us to gain insight into how to prevent errors. By protecting reporters we will stimulate a rich process that should enable providers to improve dramatically the quality of care.

The bill also establishes a new Center for Patient Safety within HHS to be the focal point of Administration policy on patient safety. This center will administer a new medical errors database of non-identifiable information that researchers will use to identify national trends and encourage best practices to prevent errors and improve health care quality.

Finally, the bill establishes a process through which new, voluntary standards for interoperability can be developed.

In our quest for improved health care quality, the urgency for investing in health care information technology is exceeded only by that for investment in patient safety systems. The health care industry has lagged far behind other sectors of our economy in adopting the information systems that can assure continuous quality improvement.

Consequently, we must not only shield the reporting of health care delivery problems from legal liability, but also support the development of the infrastructure needed to gather data, analyze them, problem solve, and disseminate recommendations for quality improvement. Therefore, the bill establishes a new technology advisory board to provide expert advice to the Secretary in creating these interoperability standards. We simply cannot afford to establish different brand information systems that do not talk to each other. Patient safety is too important!

That is what H.R. 4889 is designed to do. H.R. 4889 would facilitate the identification of health care delivery problems through voluntary and confidential reporting. It supports the analysis of data and development of recommended best practices. And it provides for the dissemination of recommendations for best practices back to the health care industry. All of these activities would be privileged—or shielded from discovery for litigation purposes—because it has been the fear of legal liability that has had such a chilling effect on the development of the reporting and analysis of errors data that can save lives and create a health care delivery system capable of continuous quality improvement.

Throughout, we also recognize the need for establishing information systems that communicate with each other to support clinical decision making as well as quality improvement activities. We were told by many experts that national leadership is needed to speed the adoption of technology standards for health care information systems. This bill establishes an advisory board and process for the development of national information technology standards and will assure the development of interoperable systems in the competitive market with tremendous benefits for quality improvement in health care.

This legislation incorporates the recommendations of experts, consumers, policymakers, and my colleagues in Congress. The overwhelming and positive response to our proposal is testimony to the broad recognition in the industry that much more can be done, and that the will is there to make it happen. I'm pleased that 50 provider, patient, quality improvement, and national accreditation organizations have endorsed this Chairman's draft.

Of course, Secretary Thompson needs no introduction to this Subcommittee. In working with you and officials from CMS, the Agency for Healthcare Research and Quality, the Department of the Treasury and the White House, we believe we have shaped a good legislative product the Administration can endorse. Mr. Secretary, I welcome you here today.

Our second panel is impressive. Dr. Lucian Leape from Harvard University is a member of the IOM's Committee on Quality of Health Care in America and an author of the 1999 report on errors. Dr. Michael Wood is the President and CEO of the Mayo Foundation and is testifying on behalf of the Healthcare Leadership Council.

Also joining us is Ken Segal, Director of the Pittsburgh Regional Healthcare Initiative, and whose organization testified at our last hearing. Dr. Herbert Pardes is the President of New York-Presbyterian and CEO of the New York-Presbyterian Healthcare System. He brings a wealth of expertise on information technology and computerized medical records.

Lastly, Jill Rosenthal is a Project Manager at the National Academy for State Health Policy who will give us a perspective from the states.

Welcome, Secretary Thompson. We look forward to your testimony.

Before I recognize Secretary Thompson, I would like to recognize my colleague, Mr. Stark.

Mr. STARK. Thank you, Madam Chair, and thank you for holding these hearings. There are, indeed, some differences out in the land of patient protection and my hope is that those can be reconciled.

I would quote here from an article from Medscape, Money, and Medicine, and it says that the approaches formed by IOM report were the basis of recommendations unveiled several years ago. This is an article in the year 2000. It says, "However, groups are sharply split over whether health care organizations should be mandated to report serious or sentinel medical events to State agencies. Such information would be grouped together and submitted to a Federal agency, which would report the data to the public while maintaining the confidentiality of the patients and health care professionals involved. Data reported to a Federal entity would be analyzed to determine why the error occurred and how to reduce or eliminate the likelihood that such an event would be repeated."

Then in March of 2000, there was an editorial in, interestingly enough, the British Medical Journal, but it was co-authored by one of our witnesses today, speaking to the issue of medical errors, and I quote from the editorial. It says, "If we can mobilize our resources and make safety our priority, health care can make tremendous strides in the next few years. Today's culture of blame and guilt too often shackles us. Achieving the culture we need, one of learning, trust, curiosity, systems thinking, and executive responsibility, will be immensely difficult. Harder still, we must now accomplish this cultural change under the spotlight of a newly aroused public that, given our track record," referring to the medical and hospital profession, "it is understandably doubtful that health care can on its own do what needs to be done."

"Indeed, the public's doubt in our commitment may be all too well founded. In truth, no other hazardous industry has achieved safety without substantial external pressure." I would like to repeat that. "No other hazardous industry has achieved safety without substantial external pressure. Three decades of accumulating evidence of medical errors offers plenty of ammunition to those who claim that we may need to be forced to do what is at bottom right."

"The need is obvious and the mandate is clear. Will we respond adequately and fast enough? Will hospitals and health care organizations get serious enough soon enough about patient safety? Will they make the changes that are needed, and will they be willing to hold themselves accountable for achieving improvements? Can we accept the legitimacy of the public's right to know when serious accidents occur and can we honor the public's legitimate expectation that we will admit our mistakes, investigate, and make changes necessary to prevent them in the future?"

"As we enter this new century, a key lesson from the old is that everyone benefits from transparency. Both the safety of our patients and the satisfaction of our workers require an open and nonpunitive environment where information is freely shared and responsibility is broadly accepted."

I am afraid, Madam Chair, that by ignoring the mandatory portion of the IOM's recommendations for medical procedures that cause death or major harm, we are dancing this jig on one leg and that the bill may need some serious adjustment, but we will hear from witnesses about that as we proceed and maybe we can help the process through the enlightenment of these hearings. Thank you.

Chairman JOHNSON. Thank you very much, Mr. Stark. I would like to recognize Chairman Thomas. I am delighted he has joined us for this important hearing, part of it, at least.

Chairman THOMAS. Thank you very much, Madam Chairman. Thank you, Mr. Secretary, for being with us. Knowing that there has been some bipartisan movement on this, I would just react partially to the Ranking Member, the gentleman from California. I know one sure recipe for disaster, and that is to continue to ignore in any legislative form trying to move forward. I know that there are multiple Committee jurisdictions. There are different ways to do this. Perhaps this will need some additional examination as we move forward, as most legislation does.

I want to compliment the Chair and this Subcommittee for beginning the process. It maybe is several years later than it should have begun, but it is beginning. I also know that there will be significant changes, hopefully, in the industry as they become more systematic and look at models that actually work and we may have to adjust the legislation to the realities of the changing work environment to produce a reduction of errors in the workplace, especially hospitals and other areas outside of hospitals. I understand there is going to be a cost, a new way of doing things.

Given the information we know we have, a non-reaction is completely unacceptable. So, I want to underscore the fact that you need to begin to finish and I believe we have begun the process, certainly not too early, and we are open to any reasonable, rational, and appropriate changes, as we always are, in driving toward the end product, which is reducing medical errors and improving patient safety.

I want to underscore the fact that the Secretary was kind enough to come, especially at a Subcommittee level, to give this a bit more impetus, because I believe although he may not agree the product is perfect the way it is and will have some suggestions as well, beginning the process is all important. I want to thank the Chairman for doing that, and thank you for allowing me to say a word. Thank you very much, Mr. Chairman.

Mr. Secretary, it is a pleasure to have you. My apologies that the business of the House on the Floor delayed the beginning of this hearing. Welcome.

STATEMENT OF HON. TOMMY G. THOMPSON, SECRETARY, U.S. DEPARTMENT OF HEALTH AND HUMAN SERVICES, ACCOMPANIED BY CAROLYN CLANCY, ACTING DIRECTOR, AGENCY FOR HEALTHCARE RESEARCH AND QUALITY

Secretary THOMPSON. Thank you very much, Madam Chairwoman, and thank you so very much for holding this hearing, and the Ranking Member, Congressman Stark, and Chairman Thomas, and all Members of the Committee, it is a pleasure to be here. Madam Chairperson, I would like to ask your permission to introduce for the record a statement from Secretary Paul O'Neill of the U.S. Department of the Treasury who has asked me to submit it, and I will. I would also like to introduce Carolyn Clancy, who is the head of AHRQ, who is going to be able to stay on after I leave in order to answer any questions, if there are still questions after I leave.

Chairman JOHNSON. Thank you. We will submit that statement.

[The statement of Secretary O'Neill follows:]

Statement of the Hon. Paul O'Neill, Secretary, U.S. Department of the Treasury

PATIENT SAFETY IMPROVEMENT ACT

Today at least 100,000 Americans every year die because of medical errors and mistakes, despite the best efforts of the good doctors, nurses and hospitals in this country. The system they work in is broken. Everybody knows a story about a friend or relative who went into the hospital and had something go wrong. We can and must change that. We've tinkered long enough with our health care system—a band-aid here, a cosmetic fix there. Mistakes and errors don't just cost money, they cost lives.

I spent considerable time working to reform the health care delivery system in Pittsburgh, where I saw firsthand that it is possible to make systematic and far-reaching improvements in health care quality and safety. Every American deserves this kind of high-quality, error free health care.

We know from other high risk industries, such as aviation, that a fundamental requirement for improvement is that it must be safe to learn from errors. Punishment, ridicule and legal exposure drive error reporting underground so corrective action does not occur. Properly constructed health care quality and safety initiatives should be protected from liability. They are not now.

Along with Secretary Thompson, our leader on national health care policy, I applaud the sponsors of the Patient Safety Improvement Act for tearing down the barriers to quality improvement so that we can move toward the goal of error-free health care for every American.

Secretary THOMPSON. Members of the Subcommittee and Madam Chairwoman. It is always good to see you, Madam Chairwoman, and to thank you for your ongoing commitment and your passion and compassion to quality health care for all Americans. I am proud to be your partner in that effort.

I am honored to appear before this very important Subcommittee today to discuss ways that the Federal Government can help reduce medical errors and improve the safety of the health care services that Americans receive.

I first testified before Congress about this issue early in my tenure as Secretary of Health and Human Services. Reducing medical errors, and doing so dramatically, is a priority for this administration.

In the last few years, the Department of Health and Human Services has developed a coordinated set of initiatives to identify and to reduce threats to patient safety and improve the quality of patient care. Yet, while these initiatives are important, they are, as the Chairman has already indicated, only a beginning.

As we all know, the Institute of Medicine's landmark 1999 report, "To Err Is Human," alerted the Nation to the patient safety challenge in ways that prior studies had not. The IOM estimated that up to 98,000 Americans die each year as a result of medical errors, making such errors the eighth leading cause of death in the United States, as you indicated, Madam Chairwoman. More people die from medical errors than from automobile accidents, breast cancer, or AIDS. While there has been subsequent debate about the actual number of deaths, the precise number is less significant than the indisputable fact that the rate of medical errors is unacceptably high.

So, for the sake of public health, much more can and must be done to eliminate the barriers that discourage health care providers from participating voluntarily and enthusiastically in local and regional patient safety and quality improvement efforts. Yet the main barrier is that professionals fear that if they report some event or some condition that is less than perfect, the report will be used to generate litigation, not redress or correct the problem.

The savings generated by national malpractice litigation reform would help us provide a prescription drug benefit for seniors and help the uninsured obtain insurance. We in the Bush Administration are doing all we can to take those steps, and we will not stop until the job is done.

One of the steps we must take is addressing your legislation, Madam Chairwoman. Without question, health care providers need assurances that if they report errors, the information will be used constructively, not as evidence in a trial. The President made this point explicit in his speech in my great home State medical college in Wisconsin when he said, and I quote, "We actually have a system that penalizes doctors for trying to prevent errors and avoid complications in patient care, because when they discuss information about patient care, they put themselves or others at a risk of a lawsuit."

I am very pleased to say that the legislation this Committee is considering, legislation that you have authored, Madam Chairwoman, for which I thank you very deeply, represents an essential change in direction, taking us away from the blame game after there has been an injury and setting us on the more productive path of improving the system and preventing adverse events from occurring in the first place. It will do so by encouraging a culture of learning and constant quality improvement in our health care system.

Of course, the vast majority of doctors, nurses, and other health care professionals are dedicated, conscientious people who work long hours under very difficult circumstances, and, in fact, health professionals are not opposed to quality improvement. Just the opposite, and you are going to hear about that this afternoon. They embrace it. As they have told all of us, it must be real, and it must be meaningful quality improvement done in a supportive and in a cooperative way. The legislation in this Committee meets these important principles, and I thank you.

Madam Chairwoman, your legislation provides the types of protections that the President believes are essential to foster the development and the institutionalization of quality improvement efforts in our health care system. I commend you and your colleagues for your leadership in developing and, we hope, enacting this very important legislation.

The proposal assures doctors and other health professionals that if they report information to expert Patient Safety Organizations, the information will be used for patient quality improvement efforts and will be kept confidential. This will encourage them to report and will greatly increase the amount of data available for analysis by the experts. Because they will receive information from more than one hospital and about more than one doctor, they will be able to detect patterns of good and bad practices that might not otherwise be noticeable on a single provider basis. They will be able to provide recommendations to local providers about system changes that the providers would not have been able to develop on their own. These new Patient Safety Organizations will promote collaboration and cooperation among providers on a regional basis. They will be proactive.

The legislation recognizes that the new ways of addressing quality are needed. It focuses on system improvements, not attacks on the providers. It will make it easier to bring information about how the system works, rather than one provider, one doctor, or even one hospital. It will be able to gather information from a broad range of providers and see how the system works and how to improve it.

Let me share with you one example of how detection of medical errors and sharing of information can bring significant changes when errors become much too extensive. Anesthesiologists have dramatically reduced the patient death rate from anesthesia administered during surgery, from 2 deaths per 10,000 anesthetics in the mid-eighties to, today, about 1 death for every 200,000 to 300,000 anesthetics administered today. How did they do it?

First, they acknowledged that a problem existed in the way the equipment was being used. They shared that information, and it changed the way anesthesiology was practiced. They standardized anesthesia machines to ensure consistency in the delivery of the drugs and also addressed issues of fatigue and sleep deprivation, changes in training, and competing institutional priorities.

Anesthesiologists have shown us what can be done by using the example in your legislation, Madam Chairwoman. It is a combination of technology, work processes, human factors, institutional culture, and the working environment.

The bill is forward-looking and proactive. The Patient Safety Organizations will be able to examine processes and look at outcomes at various institutions and make suggestions for improvements. The measure recognizes the value of local and private quality efforts. Doctors and hospitals will be able to work together with local Patient Safety Organizations to identify problems and experiment with different ways of improving care.

Madam Chairwoman, your bill also complements existing HHS patient safety activities and, in turn, will help us to guide our ongoing technical assistance to private sector initiatives in the Patient Safety Organizations. Included in these efforts is our Patient Safety Task Force, which brings together the Centers for Disease Control and Prevention, the Centers for Medicare and Medicaid Services, and the Food and Drug Administration (FDA), along with our lead research agency on patient safety, the Agency for Healthcare Research and Quality.

One of our initiatives which has been undertaken by the FDA includes our partnering with the private sector to develop new technologies, such as bar coding medications. That will produce electronic prescription programs that can be introduced widely and help diminish the number of medication errors. Bar coding is so simple. Grocery stores use it all the time. We are funding now the research to apply bar coding technology to the way that patient information is stored and reviewed and the way medications are dispensed. This is going to save money, and much more importantly, is going to save lives.

In total, the FDA is receiving $5 million in new funding for patient safety, bringing its total funding for this issue to $22 million. The new funds will allow the agency to improve its ability to assess and follow up on reports of adverse events that occur after the use of FDA-regulated products.

An important goal of the Task Force is to simplify the reporting of patient safety data to our agencies. The current system is unnecessarily burdensome. The same adverse event often needs to be reported in different ways, on separate forms, to different HHS components, and those who report the data never learn whether it is useful. The Patient Safety Task Force will replace this cumbersome system, providing a new streamlined system that uses new technologies to help collect and analyze incoming data.

Our funding request also reflects our personal commitment. Included in AHRQ's fiscal year 2003 budget submission is a request for $2 million to launch a Patient Safety Improvement Corps, experts now who will work with State health departments and health care institutions to expand State and local capacity to use existing knowledge to identify and eliminate threats to patient safety.

So, Madam Chairwoman, I look forward to working with you and all the Members on this Subcommittee on this legislation because it is not some matter of arcane public policy or some set of rules only an actuary could love. It is about saving lives, nothing more, nothing less, and that is worth our time, our energy, and our commitment.

I would be more than happy to answer any questions that you or Members of the Subcommittee might have, and I thank you very much again, Madam Chairwoman and Members, for having me here and holding this hearing on this very important subject.

[The prepared statement of Secretary Thompson follows:]

Statement of the Hon. Tommy G. Thompson, Secretary, U.S. Department of Health and Human Services

Good morning, Madam Chairwoman and members of the Subcommittee. I am honored to appear before you today to discuss ways the Federal government can help reduce medical errors and improve the safety of the health care services that Americans receive.

In the last few years the Department of Health and Human Services (HHS) has developed a coordinated set of initiatives to identify and reduce threats to patient safety and improve the quality of patient care. While these initiatives are important, they are only a beginning.

President Bush and I recognize that significant progress will only be achieved when the talents and energies of health professionals are fully engaged in improving the quality of care. We have been heartened by the recent emergence of several notable private sector patient safety initiatives. But much more needs to be done—and can be done—to eliminate the barriers that discourage health care providers from participating, voluntarily and enthusiastically, in local and regional patient safety and quality improvement efforts.

The main barrier, of course, is the fear professionals have that if they report some event or some condition that is less than perfect, their report will be used to stir up litigation rather than the fix the problem. They need assurances that if they report, the information will be used constructively, not destructively. The President made this point explicitly in his speech at the Medical College of Wisconsin, in Milwaukee, when he said, "We actually have a system that penalizes doctors for trying to prevent errors and avoid complications in patient care," because when they discuss information about patient care they put themselves, or others, at risk of a lawsuit. As the President said, "This doesn't make much sense. These good faith efforts do not deserve the punishment of a lawsuit." He called on Congress to remedy this situation.

I am pleased to say that the legislation this Committee is considering represents the change in direction that the President called for and that is essential to improving quality of care in this country. It will take us away from the blame game played after there has been an injury and will set us on the more productive path of working together to improve the system and to prevent adverse events from occurring in the first place, by encouraging a culture of learning and constant quality improvement in our health care system.

The vast majority of doctors, nurses, and other health care professionals are dedicated, conscientious people who work long hours under very difficult circumstances. They are there when we need them. They would be a critical part of our front-line defense in the event of a bio-terrorism attack. They are heroes. And we should recognize this, to them and to ourselves. We should support, not attack them.

Health professionals are not opposed to quality improvement. Just the opposite; they embrace it. We should support their efforts to improve quality. But it must be real and meaningful quality improvement, done in a supportive and cooperative way. The legislation this Committee proposes meets these important principles.

Madam Chairwoman, your legislation provides the types of protections that the President believes are essential to foster the development and institutionalization of quality improvement efforts in our health care system. I commend you, and your colleagues, for your leadership in developing, and, we hope, moving this important legislation.

The Patient Safety Challenge

The Institute of Medicine's (IOM) landmark 1999 report, *To Err is Human,* alerted the nation to the patient safety challenge in ways that prior studies had not. The IOM estimated that between 44,000 and 98,000 Americans die each year as a result of medical errors, making them the eighth leading cause of death in the United States. More people die from medical errors than from automobile accidents, breast cancer, or AIDS. While there has been subsequent debate about the actual number of deaths, it is clear that the rate of medical errors is unacceptably high.

I would like to highlight four of the IOM conclusions that are particularly relevant to today's hearing. First, the elimination of medical errors will not be accomplished by attempting to identify and discipline the "bad apples". The IOM report concludes that errors are not solely the fault of individual doctors, nurses, and other clinicians; they are often "a failure in the process of delivering care in a complex delivery system." System failures result from a complex interaction of people, technology, work processes, and working conditions, but few health care providers have expertise in the identification and analysis of contributors to system failures.

Second, the IOM report cautions that if a patient experiences an adverse event during the process of care, this does not necessarily mean that a medical error has occurred. Most medical care entails some level of risk, and there can be complications or side effects, even unforeseen ones, from the underlying condition or from the treatment itself. We should not equate problem outcomes with bad practice, but, rather, we should strive to differentiate one from the other.

Third, the IOM concluded that much can be learned from the analysis of errors—from errors that result in serious patient injury or death as well as from errors that result in little or no patient injury, but which, when aggregated, can help identify patterns of system failures. To foster such analyses, the IOM urged health care organizations to implement non-punitive systems for reporting and analyzing errors within their organizations and encouraged the development of voluntary reporting systems.

Fourth, the IOM concluded that health care providers need to be assured that if they report errors that are necessary to detect system problems, these reports will be used for that purpose in a culture of safety rather than unproductively as grist for the litigation mill. As the IOM report reminds us:

> Patient safety is also hindered through the liability system and the threat of malpractice, which discourages the disclosure of errors. The discoverability of data under legal proceedings encourages silence about errors committed or observed. Most errors and safety issues go undetected and unreported, both externally and within health care organizations.

The failure to report errors hampers quality improvement efforts and threatens the quality of care for us. It also blocks our best efforts to improve the quality of health care information systems. If providers are reluctant to keep track of the information required to improve the quality and safety of health care delivery for fear of lawsuits, health care providers will continue to lag behind in electronic information systems, despite all our work to develop effective standards and support for 21st century medical information systems. The IOM urged Congress to guaranty the confidentiality of data related to patient safety and quality improvement.

Proposed Substitute for HR 4889

Madam Chairwoman, the Administration supports your efforts to pass your proposed substitute for HR 4889, and enact legislation to remove the liability barriers to improving quality and safety of health care during this session of Congress. Your proposal appropriately responds to the IOM recommendations and advances the Administration's goal of facilitating health care professionals' ability to improve the quality of our health care.

The proposal assures doctors and other health professionals that if they report information to expert Patient Safety Organizations (PSOs), that information will be used for patient quality improvement efforts and will be kept confidential. This will encourage them to report, and will greatly increase the amount of data available for analysis by experts. Because the PSOs will receive information about more than one hospital and about more than one doctor, they will be able to detect patterns of good and bad practices that might not otherwise be noticeable on a single provider basis. They will be able to provide recommendations to local providers about system changes that the providers would not have been able to develop on their own. These new Patient Safety Organizations will promote collaboration and cooperation among providers on a regional basis. They will be proactive.

The legislation recognizes that new ways of addressing quality are needed. If we have too many deaths and injuries from medical care now, the current system—based on finding fault with individual providers—must not be working. The bill changes the focus along the lines outlined by the President, and sets the new direction he identified. There are four important elements of the bill that start us down a new and better path.

First, the legislation focuses on system improvement. Rather than focusing on finding individual "bad actors," it recognizes the fact that health care is delivered a part of a system. No person, not even a doctor, is perfect. But by looking at the system in which care is delivered, we can provide protection against human frailties. The role of the individual provider is critical, but systems can help providers, give them more information, and warn them about possible mistakes. The legislation will help identify system failures by enabling PSOs to examine a wide range and large number of providers. It will make it easier to bring information about how the system works, rather than reviewing the practices of one doctor or even one hospital. It will be able to gather information from a broad range of providers and see how the system works.

Second, the legislation is forward looking and proactive. The Patient Safety Organizations will be able to examine processes and look at outcomes at various institutions, and make suggestions for improvements. Rather than focusing only on adverse events that have occurred, they will proactively identify better ways of delivering care.

Third, it is pragmatic. It takes the common sense approach that the way to improve quality is to identify problems and make improvements. Instead of playing the blame game and litigating against our doctors for particular events that may or may not represent malpractice, the legislation recognizes the importance of preventing the adverse event from occurring in the first place.

It recognizes that more must be done to improve quality and safety. The Administration fully supports effective enforcement programs based on available data to identify "bad actors" and remove them from medical practice. Information from medical records and other existing data sources will continue to be available for plaintiffs who are injured negligently as a result of medical errors. What is desperately needed, however, is new information to help prevent errors in the first place. And that is what this bill will provide.

Finally, the bill recognizes the value of local and private quality efforts. We cannot improve quality by imposing solutions from Washington. There is often no one right way, and if there were, Washington might be the last to know about it. The best way to improve quality is to integrate it in the thoughts and processes and habits of the people who actually deliver care. Doctors and hospitals will be able to work together with local Patient Safety Organizations to identify problems and experiment with different ways of improving care.

Current HHS Activities

Madam Chairwoman, your bill also complements existing HHS patient safety activities and, in turn, will help to guide our ongoing technical assistance to private sector initiatives, including the new Patient Safety Organizations.

One of my major management initiatives at HHS has been to foster better coordination and integration of related activities that cross agency lines so that we can speak as "one Department." And we are here today as one Department, with the Centers for Medicare and Medicaid Services joining the Agency for Healthcare Research and Quality in supporting this legislation.

I am delighted to report that patient safety is an exemplary model of inter-agency coordination. We have created a Patient Safety Task Force that brings together three agencies with regulatory and data collection responsibilities—the Centers for Disease Control and Prevention, the Centers for Medicare and Medicaid Services, and the Food and Drug Administration—and our lead research agency on patient safety, the Agency for Healthcare Research and Quality. An important goal of the Task Force is to simplify the reporting of patient safety data to HHS agencies. The current system is unnecessarily burdensome. The same adverse event often needs to be reported in different ways on separate forms to different HHS components, and those who report the data never learn whether it was useful.

The Patient Safety Task Force will replace this cumbersome system in two ways. At the front end, it is creating a single computer interface and standardizing the required information so that those who are required to report this information will only have to enter the data once and will only be asked to report data that will be helpful for patient safety analyses; the computer systems will then route the information to the appropriate HHS components. At the back end, the Task Force wants to ensure that we close the "reporting loop" by ensuring that the data are integrated and analyzed and that the non-identifiable data maintained by AHRQ and the results of its research can be searched in real time by those reporting the data. Patient safety improvement can only be a true public-private sector collaboration if those who report information also benefit from its analysis. Our experience in streamlining the reporting and analysis of data will be helpful as AHRQ provides technical assistance to the Patient Safety Organizations created by your bill.

Let me now turn to specific initiatives at these agencies. With $55 million in dedicated funding in FY 2002 and a request of $60 million for FY 2003, AHRQ is now the leading funder of patient safety research in the world. Its current research portfolio includes 5 large initiatives, including support for 24 demonstration projects related to the collection, analysis, and use of patient safety data; 22 projects developing and testing state-of-the-art clinical informatics applications; 8 projects related to working conditions (such as fatigue, stress, and sleep deprivation); 23 projects fostering innovative approaches to improving patient safety; and 7 projects to develop, demonstrate, and evaluate new approaches to improving provider education related to patient safety. In addition, AHRQ will soon receive a report from the IOM on structured approaches for reporting patient safety data. That report, and the ongoing results of these and future research projects, will be shared with Patient Safety Organizations as they become operational.

AHRQ's FY 2003 budget submission requests $2 million to launch a Patient Safety Improvement Corps, experts who will work with State health departments and health care institutions to expand State and local capacity to use existing knowledge to identify and eliminate threats to patient safety. In recognition of the dearth of expertise in patient safety analysis, AHRQ will work with Patient Safety Organizations in the development of the Corps and will work to leverage existing Federal expertise across the government to ensure that these private sector initiatives can become operational as soon as possible.

As you can see, AHRQ is well positioned to carry out its proposed statutory role as a "science partner" for Patient Safety Organizations. AHRQ sees the potential for tremendous synergy between the activities of Patient Safety Organizations and its ongoing national research. Moreover, the agency has already seen tremendous public and private sector interest—from States, health care institutions, health plans, and providers—in participating in such initiatives, if only protections of the type proposed in this bill can be provided for patient safety data. As a result, this legislation will greatly enhance AHRQ's ability to carry out its patient safety mission.

The Centers for Disease Control and Prevention (CDC) is pursuing a number of patient safety initiatives, including the National Electronic Disease Surveillance System (NEDSS). NEDSS will electronically link data collected by private-sector health care organizations and public health departments. It can serve as a model for how to increase efficiency, volume, accuracy, completeness and timeliness of reporting and exchanging information. In FY 2000, CDC provided funding for 14 States to develop NEDSS systems. CDC has also provided funding for 32 States and three large metropolitan areas to assess their current health information systems and to determine how they can implement NEDSS specifications and standards. The FY 2003 budget request and the 2002 enacted level include $2 million for CDC to collect more information on hospital-acquired infections.

The Food and Drug Administration (FDA) also has several initiatives underway to improve patient safety. For example, the FY 2003 budget includes an increase of $5 million above the $17 million provided in FY 2002 for the FDA to improve the collection and analysis of adverse event data, and to ensure that response to findings is timely and well communicated. FDA is working to improve labeling and packaging standards to reduce the chances of clinicians confusing drugs with similar names or making dosage errors, both of which can lead to adverse interactions between drugs. In addition, for biological products the FDA is requiring all establishments to report any event associated with biologics that were distributed by the manufacturer, including blood, blood components, and source plasma, that represents a deviation in manufacturing. FDA is also piloting a program of active collaboration with community medical programs to collect information about product safety that will supplement information from spontaneous reporting systems. And the FDA is developing a regulation to reduce drug administration errors by having bar coding technology apply to the administration of drugs.

Further, as you are aware, the Centers for Medicare and Medicaid Services (CMS) already contracts with Quality Improvement Organizations (QIOs), formerly known as Peer Review Organizations (PROs), in each State to improve the quality of care and reduce errors through the collegial dissemination of best practices. They are accomplishing this in a number of ways, most of which are specified in our contract with the QIO. For example, CMS and the QIOs are working to improve clinical health outcomes of Medicare Beneficiaries and to prevent clinical disorders in a variety of health care settings. For instance, QIOs work with nursing homes in their states using the publicly reported Minimum Data Sets quality of care measures developed by CMS. QIOs also provide information to Medicare beneficiaries and their families, which can be used for selecting nursing homes, improving nursing home care, and obtaining a better understanding about nursing home care. Likewise, QIOs are working with home health agencies in their states, using the publicly reported OASIS quality of care measures developed by CMS. As with nursing homes, the QIOs provide information to Medicare beneficiaries and their families. QIOs also are continuing work with hospitals to reduce medication and other system failures related to acute myocardial infarction, heart failure, and pneumonia, and are adding a new clinical area focus, the prevention of surgical infection. The QIOs also focus some of their efforts on Critical Access Hospitals. Furthermore, in physician offices, QIOs are continuing work in the areas of care for chronic diseases like diabetes and preventative services like mammography and adult immunizations for flu and pneumonia. In addition to these various clinical settings, QIOs are focusing on different populations. They will continue work to eliminate health disparities between certain medically underserved populations and the general population. We also have added rural beneficiaries to the list of the groups eligible for these projects. And QIOs will continue work to ensure that Medicare+Choice Organizations are part of CMS' overall efforts to improve health outcomes and enrollee satisfaction for beneficiaries enrolled in a Medicare+Choice Organization.

In addition to clinical quality improvement, QIOs are helping to improve patient safety and health through helpful information and effective communication. The QIOs play an active role in communicating publicly reported nursing home and home health agency quality of care measures; and provide assistance to providers and beneficiaries in their states in interpreting and using this information. Additionally, through coordination with JCAHO, the QIOs are assisting hospitals in their states in developing the infrastructure and tools to permit electronic self-reporting of quality of care measures. The QIOs also are continuing to conduct those communication activities required by law, such as preparing an annual report and providing beneficiary and provider information. Additionally, QIOs are establishing a Consumer Advisory Council to advise them regarding consumer-oriented activities.

QIOs are also dedicated to improving beneficiary safety through Medicare beneficiary protection activities. The QIOs continue to provide review and beneficiary complaint responses as required by law and regulations. Additionally, the QIOs have implemented a new element of the beneficiary complaint response program utilizing the mediation process to supplement the more formal complaint review procedures. Moreover, a Payment Error Prevention Program has been revamped and included in the QIOs statement of work. Under the Hospital Payment Monitoring Review Program, the QIOs will continue to review medical records for coding and medical necessity in order to estimate national and statewide payment error rates for inpatient PPS services. Finally, CMS uses special studies to direct the QIOs to perform work or special projects that are not identified in the other tasks, but fall within the scope of our contract with them.

Patient Safety Coordination Beyond the Department

Madam Chairwoman, I also want to note that my interest in improving the coordination of patient safety activities extends beyond my own Department. I recognize that other Departments have a strong interest and activities in patient safety, and it is critical that we not work at cross purposes. We are using the existing Quality Interagency Coordination (QuIC) Task Force, which includes all Departments, agencies, and entities with an interest in improving the quality of patient care, to coordinate the overall Federal response to the IOM's report on medical errors. The QuIC has held a national summit to set the agenda on patient safety research, initiated a breakthrough series with the Institute for Healthcare Improvement to foster improvements in high-risk settings in health care facilities that the Federal government manages, and helped produce materials for dissemination to the public on steps that people can take to prevent medical errors from happening to them.

We are also working with other nations to leverage our resources and share our knowledge. On October 10, 2001, the Secretary of State for Health in the United Kingdom (UK), Alan Milburn, and I signed a cooperative agreement to support collaborative activities in quality improvement and patient safety. Already there have been positive activities between the United States (US) and the UK in the areas of adverse event reporting and patient safety research. We are working closely with the newly formed National Patient Safety Agency (NPSA) in the UK to standardize reporting formats and coordinate our research agendas. As I speak, UK and US patient safety researchers are meeting today to explore common research methods for patient safety.

Conclusion

Madam Chairwoman, I look forward to working with you on this legislation and would like to convey, once again, the President's appreciation for your leadership in this area. I would be happy to answer any questions that you may have. Thank you.

Chairman JOHNSON. Thank you very much, Secretary Thompson. I would like to just highlight, and then I will move to Members for questions, a couple of statements in your written testimony. These statements enlarge on the point that you have made very well, and that is that the point of an errors reporting system is system change, and you get system change only through a deep knowledge of lots of little things that are happening.

You say in your testimony that errors that result in little or no patient injury can be aggregated to help identify patterns of system failure. It is not just errors that result in death or injury that can help you improve the quality of the health care system. It is all those little miscellaneous things that people observe and see. Some of them are not even actions taken. They are just thoughts about how actions could be better taken or possibilities avoided, as in the case of the anesthesiologist.

You also say the best way to improve quality is to integrate quality in the thoughts, processes, and habits of the people who actually deliver care. I think those statements are extremely important. You cannot integrate quality into people's thoughts and actions if at the same time half their mind is compelled by fear.

So, the underlying issue in this bill is to put in place a system that can use all those little perceptions and experiences of the actual online, frontline care givers who provide health care to Americans. These people use from their observations and experience, whether injury is involved, whether death is involved, or whether nothing like that is involved, their knowledge and experience to improve the systems and the environment of safety in our institutions. So, I thank you for your testimony and I am going to turn to Members. Mr. Chairman, would you like to question?

Chairman THOMAS. No.

Chairman JOHNSON. Mr. Stark, would you like to question?

Mr. STARK. Thanks. Governor, welcome again. Just a couple of items here. One, it is my understanding that you or the Department is about to receive a National Quality Forum (NQF) report sometime this year and that they, I have also been informed, will have perhaps approximately 35 precise steps that should be taken to reduce medical errors, and this is a result of a study that has gone on for some time where it has taken patient safety information and reports from hospitals around the country.

Would it not be a good idea for us to not only receive that report, but the other reports that you are spending $55 million on to see if we can focus not just on the voluntary side, because in your testimony, you do indicate that the IOM suggests voluntary reporting, but whoever typed your statement left out the other part of what IOM recommends and that is the mandatory reporting system on the sentinel events that they also feel should be part of a system.

So, my sense is that what we are discussing here today is only half a loaf and your Department has a tremendous amount of information that could be used in cooperation. It is my understanding we have had no meetings with your staff to kind of coordinate where we are. I think we have learned a tremendous amount since the report in 1999 and all that this bill seems to do is release the hospitals from any liability, but we are not going forward. For example, we know, and you know, Mr. Secretary, I believe, that computerized prescribing will save lives.

Secretary THOMPSON. Absolutely. I brought it up.

Mr. STARK. I think we also know that requiring, and the only way we could do that is through a Federal law, the use of safe needles, which is going to reduce medical accidents. I think we also know, and we have got about 90 or 100 Members of Congress who subscribe that reducing mandatory overtime for professionals like nurses will have them making their rounds when they are not too tired to perform, and that could reduce errors.

So, there are a lot of things that we all know can help. In some cases, they may be worth mandating. We do that. You know, we would not have air bags in cars if we did not mandate them. If we waited for the auto industry to do it, you and I would still be wondering about that.

So, what I guess I am saying is, could we not come together with the information that you have that you are about to receive and broaden the scope of this to really come up with a Federal policy that would not hurt the States, who some States are ahead of us.

Secretary THOMPSON. That is right.

Mr. STARK. Some States have a combination, and some are having trouble. I would hate to forestall that or preempt it by doing really too little. So, I guess my question is, would it not be a good idea for us to wait and work together to bring all of the research that—and I am not talking a long time, I am talking a couple of months and you are going to have this information, and then we could pick and sort and decides what needs legislation, what you can do administratively, and expand on the Chairman's initial step in this direction.

Secretary THOMPSON. Thank you, Congressman. I would like to respond by first thanking you for your interest in the subject, Congressman Stark, and secondly to tell you that you know quality improvement is not a static event. It is going to be an ongoing thing, and no matter what we do today, we are going to have to continue to address it in the future.

I am a big believer in accumulating the data and then acting, but AHRQ has been working on this under John Eisenberg, under his late leadership, which had been exemplary.

Mr. STARK. Right.

Secretary THOMPSON. I have worked with him on many things. This is a cause celebre for AHRQ and for the Department. We want to move, and we think that this is a giant step forward, Congressman Stark, and that is why we think the Congress should act.

We think that this proposal is a step in the right direction. There are going to be further steps, as you have indicated. A lot of the steps you have indicated, I could strongly support and believe that Congress should act in the future. This one, I do not think we should delay taking action on this one because I think it is so important. I think it needs to be done and this is a first step.

Second, bar coding is something that we need to do. Grocery stores have it. Why do we not have it in the hospitals and clinics?

Third, I would strongly suggest we take some of the fraud and abuse money and put it into a mini-Hill-Burton law for use for new technology for doctors and clinics. We would be able to solve a lot of the problems if we did that.

There are so many things out there, but as you know much more so than I do, Congressman Stark, that at the end of the session, you try and get as much done as possible. I think this is doable. I think we should do it. It is a good step, and I would like to urge your support, Congressman.

Mr. STARK. Do you think that there is any danger that this bill could preempt the States that now have mandatory reporting and frustrate their efforts to do that?

Secretary THOMPSON. I do not, because 44 States right now across the country, including my home State of Wisconsin and your State of California and your former home State of Wisconsin, have peer review. This is an extension of peer review, because in most of those 44 States, they have put into the law that the peer review conference in the work product is not admissible into court. Not every one of them is the same, but the City of Washington, DC, probably has got the best law on the books in regards to that.

So, I do not think it would in any way deter what the States are doing. In fact, I think it would encourage States to adopt further progress in quality improvement. We need it. We need quality improvement, especially in the health care field, and I think with technology and with the Patient Safety Organizations, we are going well down that road to helping to improve it and that is what I would strongly urge this Congress to take.

Mr. STARK. You would have no objection to States that require, in addition, mandatory reporting, in addition to whatever we do?

Secretary THOMPSON. I have none whatsoever. I am a big States' righter and if they want to do it, fine with them.

Chairman JOHNSON. Mr. Crane?

Mr. CRANE. Thank you, Madam Chairman. Mr. Secretary, in your testimony, you state that Quality Improvement Organizations (QIO) in each State are currently working to improve the quality of care and reduce errors through the collegial dissemination of best practices. What interaction would the Quality Improvement Organizations have with the PSOs, and how would the QIOs interpret and use the data collected by the PSOs?

Secretary THOMPSON. I think they can work very collaboratively, Congressman Crane, and they could be synergistically connected. I think that Patient Safety Organizations are going to be much broader and are going to allow for much more systemic changes in the delivery of the medical system and improvement of quality.

What is happening at the State level is more a collegial peer review kind of thing, and I believe that Quality Improvement Organizations are also of that category. The Patient Safety Organizations are going to be, I think, much broader and are going to allow for us to look at much more regional operations and hospitals and doctors and find out, you know, maybe small mistakes that, accumulated, could be changed and you could really have an impact on the system, like the anesthesiologists did.

They found that in half the hospitals—I do not know if half, but a good share of the hospitals, you turn the nozzles one way to get the anesthesia out, and in other hospitals, they turn the other way, causing a lot of mistakes. They looked at it, and they examined it, and in standardizing it, they now have been able to reduce the number of deaths from 1 out of 10,000 to 20,000 to now 1 out of 200,000 to 300,000. So, it is a tremendous improvement. We think we can do the same way with this legislation.

Mr. CRANE. Quality Improvement Organizations might use the data collected by Patient Safety Organizations to inform Medicare beneficiaries of the level of care provided in certain areas without establishing best practice guidelines, is that not correct?

Secretary THOMPSON. Well, that is entirely correct, but we just hope the latter is that they will develop best practices. This is the reason we are going to, because we think that this legislation is going to encourage best practices. We think that by setting this up and allowing this regional collection of data and being able to solve, hopefully, the problems, that this is going to establish standards that will create best practices, and that is what we are hoping is going to be the net result of this legislation.

Mr. CRANE. That is the hope of all of us and best of luck to you.

Secretary THOMPSON. I know it is.

Mr. CRANE. Thank you.

Secretary THOMPSON. Thank you, Congressman Crane.

Chairman JOHNSON. Mr. English?

Mr. ENGLISH. Thank you, Madam Chair, and thank you, Mr. Secretary, for taking on what I think is a very difficult issue and testifying on behalf of what I think has been a very fine bill that the Chairman has spent a lot of time on and has produced.

I wonder with regard, as we try to create this regime to deal with the problem of medical errors, how important is it to have standards that are flexible enough to allow for new innovations in health care that are workable in a variety of settings, and do you feel that this bill meets that standard?

Secretary THOMPSON. We do, and to answer your second question first, we do believe it does. Second, we believe that standards should be flexible enough to allow for new innovations.

You, Congressman English, have been a leader in innovations in the medical field for as long as you have been in Congress and I applaud you for that. The only way you move ahead, especially in the delivery of health care systems, is by innovating. With the changing technology and the changing science out there, you have to allow for that. The embryonic stem cells, the research that is going to come out of that, is going to be something that is going to, hopefully, provide for new therapies, and you have got to provide for that. There is new technology out there that is going to help to deliver and, hopefully, save the medical delivery system in America. It is going to have to be allowed to be able to be modified and changed and improved, all of these things.

So, you want to make sure that the standards are there, but also to allow for the flexibility to provide for innovation. That is what this country is all about, and especially in the field of medicine, which everybody is looking for the new therapy, the new drug, the new technology that is going to help cure the maladies and also improve the safety of patients.

Mr. ENGLISH. Thank you, Mr. Secretary. Madam Chair, I will yield back the balance of my time.

Chairman JOHNSON. Thank you, Mr. English. Mr. McDermott?

Mr. MCDERMOTT. Thank you, Madam Chair. I come at this with sort of a personal feeling about it, having worked in the days when you worked 36 hours on and 12 off. I have some feeling about medical errors and what may bring it about. One of the reasons I think this bill of nursing is one of those things we could do, I think mandatory overtime ought to be something that we prohibit.

I go beyond that. I have also worked on Peer Review Organizations (PRO). I have gone into hospitals all over Washington State and I discovered the best way to figure out who the bad doctors were was to go down and talk to the head nurse in the operating room and she could tell you in about 2 minutes what was going on in that hospital. The PROs and that whole operation was an attempt.

We in Washington State now have a situation of mandatory reporting of major mistakes that have caused death or major problems, and that is still discoverable in a lawsuit. One of the things, I am not clear on what you are saying. I do not think you want anything to be discoverable, and in some way, we have got to solve that problem, because if there has been an accident or an injury or some kind of problem in the hospital, someone has a right to have reimbursement or to have a settlement——

Secretary THOMPSON. Sure.

Mr. MCDERMOTT. So, you have got to be able to get the data, but if somebody says, well, this has been reported as an incident in our voluntary system, it is exempted by Federal law from being discovered, you prohibit the resolution of a case, it seems to me.

I am sure you have thought of it, and I do not want you in a Federal law to override what we have set up in the State of Washington. You said it will not preempt the State of Washington. I am not sure if that is correct.

Secretary THOMPSON. That depends upon how the law is written.

Mr. MCDERMOTT. Yes, I understand, but I think it is one of those issues we have to clarify. The larger question is, if you make it all voluntary and then protect it with secrecy—the IOM did not suggest that. They said reportable incidents are protected, but when it comes to a death or more serious—they sort of distinguish between significant events and near-misses. Explain to me how, if you protect it all by Federal law, any of it is ever going to be discovered, if you treat it simply as an issue of improvement of care.

Secretary THOMPSON. You have thrown out several things. If I could try and respond to several of them, I will try, Congressman.

Mr. MCDERMOTT. I am sorry if my question was unclear. I am not a lawyer.

[Laughter.]

Secretary THOMPSON. First off, in regards to nursing, I think that we have to do a heck of a lot more to encourage young people to go into the nursing and all health fields, and I thank you for your leadership and all of the Congresspeople in regards to the bipartisan legislation in nursing improvements. It was well thought out, it was well executed, and I appreciate it.

Mr. MCDERMOTT. Would you mind if it was part of this legislation?

Secretary THOMPSON. Pardon?

Mr. MCDERMOTT. Would you mind if we made this as an amendment to this legislation, the prohibiting of mandatory overtime?

Secretary THOMPSON. That is not for me to say, sir. I am talking about the nursing professions, encouraging people to get into it and the funding of nurses to go into teaching.

Mr. MCDERMOTT. Okay.

Secretary THOMPSON. Second, in regards to the litigation, there is nothing in this proposal that would prevent anything being discovered that is discoverable today. It is only the extension, only the material that goes to the PSOs would not be discoverable.

If, in fact, there is an underlying record that could be subpoenaed into court, you could still subpoena the nurse who is at the hospital. You could still subpoena the doctor and take depositions of those individuals. That is all discoverable. Nothing in this legislation would prevent anything that takes place currently in a Federal lawsuit to not be permitted. Only the extra step, the step of quality improvement, the step from getting the information collected from the incidents and from the various hospitals, that would be privileged and that would not be discoverable.

Mr. MCDERMOTT. If that is true, why not make it mandatory that it be done? I understand that you do not like—I understand the philosophy of government that does not like to make the government force people to do things, but it seems to me in this issue that if you make it mandatory, since it is still discoverable and people are protected on that side, I do not see why anybody would not want to have that information gathered for hospitals to look at their system and discover a more good way for the patients.

Secretary THOMPSON. I am fairly certain, Congressman, that once you start this, that is going to be the normal course of business, that even without requiring mandatory, it is going to be considered as a good health field, good health process to be able to do this, and I think you are going to encourage more to get started in this. I think that is what the Chairperson is looking for, is to get more buy-in. By doing it voluntary, I think you are getting a lot more initial buy-in, and then by that time, I think it is just going to be a normal course of business, and everybody is going to do it.

Mr. MCDERMOTT. I wish I had your faith.

Secretary THOMPSON. I am an Irishman, Congressman. I am very optimistic. I only wish you were as optimistic as I was, sir. [Laughter.]

Mr. MCDERMOTT. I yield back the balance of my time.

Chairman JOHNSON. Thank you. Congresswoman Thurman?

Mrs. THURMAN. Thank you, Madam Chairman. Thank you for having this hearing today. I know that we have worked hard to try to come up with a piece of legislation and move it along. In saying that, I do think that there have been some issues that we have raised and certainly some that Mr. McDermott just questioned and talked about were of some concerns to us. In saying that, and I do not know if, Mr. Secretary, you have seen the letter from the National Academy for State Health Policy——

Secretary THOMPSON. I do not think I have.

Mrs. THURMAN. I will make sure you get a copy of this, because it is somewhat alarming to me. We have 20 States now, I believe, that are already doing a mandatory reporting system, and what they say here is that we actually, or IOM went out and said to these States, you need to do this. We have asked you to do this, and we particularly are concerned about collecting and standardizing information about adverse events that result in death or serious harm.

I think that in this particular bill we are looking at, we really have no standards. We do not talk about whether it is harmful, how harmful. We really do not go into much detail. It just seems to be all information. So, I think there is a real concern that we will usurp what has happened in the States.

I remember when we first started these hearings back in 1996, when Chairman Thomas was the Chairman of the Subcommittee, we had several people come in and talk to this Committee and one of the things that they used in their testimony was actually the program that had been set up in Florida and I am very concerned that we may end up in a result not making this mandatory or, in fact, usurping what they are doing. In their estimation, the public is given some safeguards by having this, including to the point where they have a website that people can go look and see what is going on. So that, I think, is a real question for us in this, and I do believe that is a debatable question and it has been debate with and among this Committee over the last couple of months, trying to figure out how we could move forward. I am interested in——

Secretary THOMPSON. Do you not think, Congresswoman Thurman, we could work that out? Do you not think that we could work out the legislation with the Chairwoman——

Mrs. THURMAN. Mr. Secretary——

Secretary THOMPSON. And the Department and get something that is compatible?

Mrs. THURMAN. That——

Secretary THOMPSON. I think we all want to move in that direction and get it done and——

Mrs. THURMAN. I am not questioning that, and as I said, I think the Chairwoman, if you would have seen the bill we started with to where we are, she has worked very diligently and has worked at this. This just happens to be an issue——

Secretary THOMPSON. Yes, I understand.

Mrs. THURMAN. That sometimes you just do not come to some conclusion, and quite frankly, and we have had those conversations, I would have a very difficult time supporting something that did not track what my own State legislature put in——

Secretary THOMPSON. I understand.

Mrs. THURMAN. That is to say that I think she has done a fabulous job in this. There is another area that you mentioned, I think, a little bit in your testimony, or not in your testimony but in conversation, I think, maybe with Mr. English, on the technology part, that we should use fraud and abuse dollars to help pay for some of this. What I would like to know is, because in this bill there are no dollars to help——

Secretary THOMPSON. Right.

Mrs. THURMAN. In a bill that Mr. Houghton and I introduced, we had money in that piece of legislation to, in fact, help. Can you, in fact, then carry this out administratively?

Secretary THOMPSON. No, I cannot.

Mrs. THURMAN. Okay. So we need to figure out a way——

Secretary THOMPSON. Congresswoman, I have been talking about this for a long time. I really—it bothers me immensely as Secretary of Health and Human Services to walk into a grocery store and know that a grocery store is more technologically advanced than a lot of our hospitals and clinics across America. When I talk to people in the health field, hospital administrators and so on, and they say the cost is so much that they cannot afford it because the changing of the technology, it is antiquated by the time they get it in and, therefore, they do not want to make the investments.

So, I believe that we should have some sort of a demonstration fund. I think we can get to a paperless system in hospitals, and I have been talking about that for a long time, so that you could use your technology to get in and you would reduce the rates. If we could somehow use—the fraud and abuse money, I know, is—I am talking for myself now, nobody else—I just think it would be something that the medical profession would really rally around and say, you know, people that have done something wrong, we take money away from them, but instead of wasting, or not wasting money, but putting the money someplace else, identify the money to do something to improve the system.

Mrs. THURMAN. You and I agree. I mean, that is why when we wrote the piece of legislation we did, we figured that, I mean, not only for large hospitals, but a lot of rural hospitals who are going to be affected by this. Let me just say two things at the end of this.

Secretary THOMPSON. Okay.

Mrs. THURMAN. Number one—I do not know, which do I do? Do I give the good or the bad first? I was really not very happy with the Graduate Medical Education issue on psychology, again. I mean, it was something this Committee worked on, had worked on, had been a proposed rule, had gone through its time period, and still we are back where we were 4 years ago. You know my feelings about that.

Secretary THOMPSON. I know you——

Mrs. THURMAN. The good news is, I do want to thank you very much for the dollars that you just gave to Florida on the Ron Silver prescription drug for our low-income seniors. We do appreciate what you have done in that, and also the demonstration programs on some of the HMO Medicare+Choice things, so——

Secretary THOMPSON. We are trying a lot of demonstration programs, and on the psychologists, well, let us keep working on it.

Mrs. THURMAN. I would like something more than that, but we will talk about it.

Secretary THOMPSON. Thank you.

Mrs. THURMAN. Thank you.

Secretary THOMPSON. Thank you very much, and thank you.

Chairman JOHNSON. Thank you very much, Mr. Secretary. I know you have to leave and I appreciate your being here. I think we have completed our questions and we have kept the other panel waiting so long.

I do want to announce two things. First of all, we did just get a letter from Florida and the Greater New York area and they have very positive things to say about the voluntary reporting requirements and the interoperability standards, so we will be working on that.

Mrs. THURMAN. Madam Chairman, I know that, but I also would go back to the letter that I think the State health people said, and that was that we also need to look at the breadth of that, because they are working well.

Chairman JOHNSON. We will on the succeeding panel have a chance to ask those questions in regard to State issues.

We have a 15-minute vote. We have about 5 minutes left before that concludes. Then we have two 5-minute votes, so we will reconvene at 1:00 with the final panel. Thank you very much.

Before I recess the Committee, I am going to insert the statement of Bill Coyne for the record. Congressman Coyne has asked permission to insert his statement.

[The statement of Mr. Coyne follows:]

Statement of the Hon. William J. Coyne, a Representative in Congress from the State of Pennsylvania

I am pleased that the Ways and Means Health Subcommittee has chosen to hold a hearing on medical errors. I have been concerned about the medication error aspect of this problem for quite some time. All medical errors are unacceptable, and the Federal government must work with the health care industry toward the goal of dramatically reducing such errors.

In 1993, Steve Twedt of the Pittsburgh Post-Gazette did a series of articles on medication errors. The Pittsburgh Post-Gazette reported that the newspaper's study of 250 hospital pharmacists across the country produced an estimate of 16,000 medication errors in the surveyed institutions in 1992, with 106 of these errors causing patient deaths. Some of these errors were made by physicians, some by hospital personnel, some by pharmacists, and some by patients.

The Post-Gazette reports offered clear evidence that a significant number of people die or become ill every year because of medication errors. Furthermore, David Work, the Executive Director of the North Carolina Board of Pharmacy, testified at a Ways and Means hearing on medication errors in 1995 that "about 10,000 deaths occur nationwide from pharmaceuticals each year." There was certainly no doubt that the system for monitoring medication errors had to be improved.

In 1993, I introduced The Safe Medications Act. This legislation would have required that deaths due to the prescribing, dispensing or administering of drugs be reported by the health care facility in which the error occurred to the U.S. Pharmacopeia, a private non-profit organization directed by Congress to set drug standards. Health care institutions covered by this bill included pharmacies, hospitals, long-term care facilities, ambulatory care facilities and physician offices. Reports would have had to be made within 10 working days from the date the error was discovered. The Secretary of Health and Human Services would have worked with the U.S. Pharmacopeia and appropriate health care provider associations to notify and alert health care providers and manufacturers of potential problems. Information reported to U.S. Pharmacopeia would have remained confidential. I re-introduced this legislation in subsequent Congresses.

In 1998, U.S. Pharmacopeia unveiled a voluntary reporting system for all errors, not just those resulting in death. Health care providers report the errors and U.S. Pharmacopeia organizes them into a searchable database. They also notify health professionals about the most common medication errors and their causes. This voluntary initiative constituted a commendable first step in reducing the number of deaths caused by medical errors.

In 1999, the Institute of Medicine released the report, To Err is Human. The study described a fractured health care system that is prone to errors and detrimental to safe patient care. While this report prompted some debate on the issue, Federal legislation to reduce medical errors has not yet been enacted.

In 1999, I joined my colleague Congressman Cardin in introducing the Medicare Chronic Disease Prescription Drug Benefit Act of 1999. This legislation would have provided for a chronic disease prescription drug benefit under the Medicare Program. Furthermore, it contained language that would have ensured that appropriate safety mechanisms were in place to prevent medication errors in this program. The legislation would have directed the Secretary of Health and Human Services to establish a model for comprehensive educational programs to assure appropriate prescribing, dispensing, and use of such covered drugs. Unfortunately, Congress has failed to act on Medicare prescription drug legislation as well.

Finally, I want to thank the Pittsburgh Regional Healthcare Initiative for their hard work in reducing medical errors in Southwestern Pennsylvania and for coming today to share their experience.

The issue of medical errors is of great importance and urgency. Thousands of lives are—literally—on the line. I am pleased to see that the Ways and Means Health Subcommittee is exploring this issue, and I hope that the Ways and Means Health Subcommittee and Full Committee will work together in a bipartisan fashion to find a prompt solution to this growing problem.

Chairman JOHNSON. Congressman Stark has asked permission to insert an editorial, "Safe Health Care: Are We Up To It?" for the record.

[The information follows:]

British Medical Journal
March 18, 2002

Editorials
Safe health care: are we up to it?

We have to be

In the 8 months since we put out the call for papers for this special issue of the BMJ devoted to medical errors, the landscape has changed considerably. In Britain the Bristol Inquiry has continued to focus professional and public attention on patient safety in a manner unprecedented both for its depth and for the extent of professional involvement.[1] In the United States the recent publication of the report To Err is Human by the Institute of Medicine of the National Academy of Sciences[2] received extraordinary media coverage as well as prompt responses to its recommendations from the President and Congress.[3]

The error prevention "movement" has clearly accelerated. As the papers in this issue bear witness, major changes are occurring in the way we think about and carry out our daily work. For practicing physicians, some of the ideas and practices described here may be mind bending, or at least mind stretching. But most of the

---

[1] www.bristol-inquiry.org.uk/brisphase2.htm; accessed 6 March 2000.

[2] Kohn LT, Corrigan JM, Donaldson MS, eds. To err is human. Building a safer health system. Washington, DC: National Academy Press, 1999.

[3] Charatan F. Clinton acts to reduce medical mistakes. BMJ 2000; 320: 597 [Full Text].

insights and solutions will, we think, have resonance for all those who strive to provide safe care for patients. All physicians, after all, have had the unwelcome experience of becoming what Wu calls "the second victim," being involved in an error or patient injury and feeling the attendant sense of guilt or remorse as responsible professionals.[4] Familiar, too, are Helmreich's findings that doctors, like pilots, tend to overestimate their ability to function flawlessly under adverse conditions, such as under the pressures of time, fatigue, or high anxiety.[5]

Some of the solutions reported here are as simple as teaching emergency room doctors to read x ray films[6]; others require substantial capital investment.[7] The new world of automation described by Bates and by Gaba seems ever closer,[8 9] and, although every new technology will inevitably introduce new forms of error, it is high time for medicine to enter the computer age. We should now hope that the death knell has at last been sounded for the handwritten paper prescription; and the paper medical record, a dinosaur long overdue for extinction, may at last be en route to replacement by far more useful and reliable automated systems.

But, several of these authors warn us, making the more fundamental and lasting changes that will have a major impact on patient safety is much more difficult than simply installing new technologies. There are no "quick fixes." We must re-examine all that we do and redesign our many and complex systems to make them less vulnerable to human error.[10 11] The necessary changes are as much cultural as technical. Creating a culture of safety requires attention not only to the design of our tasks and processes, but to the conditions under which we work—hours, schedules and workloads; how we interact with one another; and, perhaps most importantly, how we train every Member of the healthcare team to participate in the quest for safer patient care.

We have already learnt a great deal from the early experiences of error reduction in healthcare organizations. First, we have discovered an immense reservoir of creativity and motivation among healthcare workers of all kinds. When given the opportunity to help, when the barriers of shame and punishment are removed, doctors, nurses, pharmacists, and others eagerly work to improve safety, implementing best practices or developing new ones.

Secondly, we have learnt again that leadership is an essential ingredient of success in the search for safety, as it is throughout the enterprise of quality improvement. In the absence of commitment from professional and organizational leaders, efforts will be fragmentary and uncoordinated and will have only minor effects. We need leadership at all levels. While local "champions"—individual doctors, pharmacists, or nurses—can, by their enthusiasm, motivate others to make improvements, major systems changes require direction and support from the top—leaders who communicate their own commitment by insisting on safety as an explicit organizational goal backed by adequate resources. The test, as Reinertsen tells us, is that senior managers feel personally responsible for each error.[12]

Thirdly, we have learnt that the problem of medical error is not fundamentally due to lack of knowledge. Though clearly we have much more to learn about how to make our systems safe, we already know far more than we put into practice. Simple measures of known effectiveness, such as unit dosing, marking the correct side before surgery on paired organs, and 24 hour availability of pharmacists and emergency physicians, are often ignored. Health care alone refuses to accept what other hazardous industries recognized long ago: safe performance cannot be expected from workers who are sleep deprived, who work double or triple shifts, or whose job designs involve multiple competing urgent priorities. Based on currently available knowledge, constructive, effective changes to improve patient safety can begin at once.

---

[4] Wu A. Medical error: the second victim. BMJ 2000; 320: 726–727 [Full Text].

[5] Helmreich RL. On error management: lessons from aviation. BMJ 2000; 320: 781–785 [Full Text].

[6] Espinosa JA, Nolan TW. Reducing errors made by emergency physicians in interpreting radiographs: longitudinal study. BMJ 2000; 320: 737–740 [Abstract/Full Text].

[7] Nightingale PG, Adu D, Richards NT, Peters M. Implementation of rules based computerised bedside prescribing and administration: intervention study. BMJ 2000; 320: 750–753 [Abstract/Full Text].

[8] Bates DW. Using information technology to reduce rates of medication errors in hospitals. BMJ 2000; 320: 788–791 [Full Text].

[9] Gaba DM. Anaesthesiology as a model for patient safety in health care. BMJ 2000; 320: 785–788 [Full Text].

[10] Reason J. Human error: models and management. BMJ 2000; 320: 768–770 [Full Text].

[11] Nolan TW. System changes to improve patient safety. BMJ 2000; 320: 771–773 [Full Text].

[12] Reinertsen JL. Let's talk about error. BMJ 2000; 320: 730 [Full Text].

If we can mobilize our resources and make safety our priority, health care can make tremendous strides in the next few years. But today's culture of blame and guilt too often shackles us. Achieving the culture we need—one of learning, trust, curiosity, systems thinking, and executive responsibility—will be immensely difficult. Harder still, we must now accomplish this cultural change under the spotlight of a newly aroused public that, given our track record, is understandably doubtful that health care can, on its own, do what needs to be done. Indeed, the public's doubt in our commitment may be all too well founded. In truth, no other hazardous industry has achieved safety without substantial external pressure. Safe industries are, by and large, highly regulated. Health care's track record of failure to act on over three decades of accumulating evidence of medical errors offers plenty of ammunition to those who claim that we may need to be forced to do what is, at bottom, right.

The need is obvious, and the mandate is clear. Will we respond adequately and fast enough? Will hospitals and healthcare organizations get serious enough, soon enough, about patient safety? Will they make the changes that are needed, and will they be willing to hold themselves accountable for achieving improvements? Can we accept the legitimacy of the public's right to know when serious accidents occur, and can we honor the public's legitimate expectation that we will admit our mistakes, investigate them, and make the changes necessary to prevent them in the future? As we enter the new century, a key lesson from the old is that everyone benefits from transparency. Both the safety of our patients and the satisfaction of our workers require an open and non-punitive environment where information is freely shared and responsibility broadly accepted.

Are we ready to change? Or will we procrastinate and dissemble—to lament later when the inevitable regulatory backlash occurs? It may seem to some that the race for patient safety has just begun, but the patience of the public we serve is already wearing thin. They are asking us to promise something reasonable, but more than we have ever promised before: that they will not be harmed by the care that is supposed to help them. We owe them nothing less, and that debt is now due.

Lucian L Leape
Adjunct Professor of Health Policy
Harvard School of Public Health, Harvard University
Boston, MA 02115, USA

Donald M Berwick
Chief Executive Officer
Institute for Healthcare Improvement
Boston, MA 02215, USA

Chairman JOHNSON. The Committee stands in recess.

[Recess.]

Chairman JOHNSON. The Subcommittee will come to order. My apologies to the panel for the delays. These things are beyond our control. Thank you. We will begin with Dr. Leape of the Harvard School of Public Health. Thank you for yours and Dr. Berwick's help, and of others from the Committee as we have developed this legislation. I appreciate it.

STATEMENT OF LUCIAN L. LEAPE, M.D., ADJUNCT PROFESSOR OF HEALTH POLICY, HARVARD SCHOOL OF PUBLIC HEALTH, HARVARD UNIVERSITY, CAMBRIDGE, MASSACHUSETTS

Dr. LEAPE. Thank you, Madam Chairman, and Mr. Stark, Members of the Committee, for the opportunity to meet with you, and thank you, Madam Chairman, for your leadership in safety. We all appreciate it and look forward to working with you.

I think it is fair to say that in spite of all the gloomy news, progress in patient safety in the past few years has really been astounding. There has been an incredible amount of activity since the Institute of Medicine report came out now not quite 3 years ago; not as much as we would like, never as fast as we would like, but significant progress nonetheless. Hospitals are changing their systems, particularly in medication systems. Hundreds have reorganized what they do. Health care systems throughout the country are leading in systems change. Regulators are intensifying their efforts. Coalitions have sprung up in many States, bringing together stakeholders to work on safety. I think there is no question safety has become a priority in health care and it is about time.

The Federal Government, I think, has played an important role in this and the proposed legislation, I believe, will expand that in the proper way. I would like to comment on just several aspects of it briefly.

The first, the Center for Patient Safety, I think is very important. The Agency for Health Care Research and Quality has been the leading force in the safety movement. Under John Eisenberg's outstanding leadership, the agency became exactly what the Institute of Medicine visualized, a central focus, a symbol of national commitment for patient safety. It is government at its best, not telling doctors how to practice, but providing them the tools they need to do better what they want to do. You should be very proud of that. I strongly recommend that you assure its future by incorporating it in this legislation as proposed.

I would like to make one comment about funding. Sixty-million dollars sounds like a lot of money. It is not. It is a drop in the bucket. Congress has wisely over the years expanded the funding for the National Institutes of Health, which we all support and which has been responsible for the dramatic advances in science over the last 20 years that has so much improved health care. But congress has never funded the equally important task of evaluating those advances.

We spend over $25 billion for the National Institutes of Health. We should spend at least 5 percent of that on developing the evidence of how those advances work. Five percent would be $1.25 billion a year. That should be the budget for AHRQ, and 20 or 30 percent of that should be earmarked for safety.

The second part of the legislation which I would like to support is the proposal to develop interoperability standards for information technology. Dr. Pardes will address this in more detail, but I would like to make several comments.

The first is that the idea of the computerized patient record has been before us in health care for over 40 years. We were talking about it when I was in medical school, and yet it has still eluded us. The benefits are obvious. For example, if you were taken to an emergency room in a hospital in a town 1,000 miles from home, they could retrieve your record, in minutes, find out what medications you were taking, what medications you are allergic to, and so forth, and give you proper treatment. The computerized record would eliminate many of the serious communication barriers that are behind many of the errors and injuries that we see in health care. It would enable patients and doctors to access their information readily, and I think it would make a tremendous difference. It would also provide the data we need for the evidence for evidence-based medicine, again, something we need to move on with. We could discover, for example, complications from a new drug within months, instead of years as at the present time. So, I strongly urge you to pass those sections. I think the time has come.

Clearly, the contentious part of the legislation has to do with the protection of voluntary reporting. Since the legislation does not address mandatory reporting, I will not either, but we can talk about that if desired. I think that no one questions the need for enhancing voluntary reporting. We all realize that sharing of information, learning from one another, is critical for improving safety.

No reporting system will succeed unless it is safe. Safe means that when you report something, you are not at risk for being punished, for being sanctioned or being involved in a malpractice suit. At the present time, peer review statutes protect reporting *within* hospitals, but that protection is lost when the report leaves the hospital walls. This bill addresses that issue and is, I think, appropriate, timely, and necessary. I do not share the concerns that it will interfere with the mandatory reporting systems or other reporting systems presently available.

I do think, however, that section 1182(D)(2) essentially nullifies the advantages that the bill provides. Removing protection for disciplinary proceedings is essentially removing protection. No right-thinking physician or nurse will talk about an error they have made if that remains in the bill because they will still be at risk. So, I think if you leave that in, you might as well not pass the legislation. I urge you to strike section 1182(D)(2). Thank you very much.

[The prepared statement of Dr. Leape follows:]

Statement of Lucian L. Leape, M.D., Adjunct Professor of Health Policy, Harvard School of Public Health, Harvard University, Cambridge, Massachusetts

I wish to lend my strong support for the proposed Amendment to H.R. 4889 offered by Mrs. Johnson, provided it is amended to provide full protection from discovery for voluntarily reported patient safety data.

Progress in patient safety over the past two years has been astounding. Virtually every national organization and all hospitals are changing their practices to reduce hazards of patient injury. Many of those efforts have been facilitated by the strong leadership provided by the Agency for Healthcare Research and Quality. While progress is never as fast as one would wish, injury rates have been reduced, and the pace of improvement is accelerating.

The proposed legislation addresses three important issues related to improving patient safety. Two of these, Section 1183, establishing a Center for Patient Safety within the Agency for Healthcare Research and Quality (AHRQ), and Section 1184, developing interoperability standards for health care information technology systems, are broadly supported; the third, protection for reporting, is more controversial. Let me comment on the easy ones first.

Center for Patient Safety within the Agency for Healthcare Research and Quality (AHRQ)

As I indicated in my testimony to the Senate Committee on Health, Education, Labor and Pensions last year, the Agency's role in advancing patient safety has been exemplary. With generous support from Congress, and under the outstanding leadership of the late John Eisenberg, AHRQ brought together diverse stakeholders to define areas in safety needing further research, disseminate information on known safe practices (such as medication safety), provided help for consumers, and requested and funded research proposals addressing a broad range of safety questions, including such diverse and important topics as the design and evaluation of reporting systems, improvement of medication systems, enhancing collaboration and teamwork, and the effect of working conditions on safe performance. It commissioned the National Quality Forum to convene a panel that developed a standard list of serious reportable events that states may use in their mandatory reporting systems, and an expert panel that will soon release a list of safety practices.

In a very short time, the Agency has become what the IOM called for, and health care has desperately needed, both a central focus of activity in safety and a demonstration of a national commitment to safety that facilitates work at the local level, in hospitals and health care organizations. This is government at its best: not telling doctors and hospitals how to practice, but providing the research, resources and information needed for them to do what they need and want to do, make health care safe for all citizens. AHRQ is now the major force for improving patient safety, and with continuing support it can become even more useful. You should be very proud of this.

I strongly recommend that the Center for Patient Safety be given your endorsement through the proposed legislation establishing it as a permanent Center within AHRQ.

The initial funding of $50 million provided by Congress in fiscal year 2001 for the safety effort at AHRQ not only gave a "jump start" to safety research—over 90 projects in six areas—it has had another very important effect: it has attracted a number of talented researchers and practitioners to work in patient safety. This is particularly important at this time because this young field of health care safety has only a handful of experts. Developing that expertise, which is analogous to specialty training in medicine, will take time, but a good beginning has been made. It is, however, just a start. The number needed is huge: providing just one qualified person in each hospital, for example, requires nearly 5000. If the momentum and commitment are to be sustained, funding for the Center for Patient Safety must be increased substantially each year.

Developing interoperability standards for health care information technology systems

Few technological advances have been so long in coming as the electronic (computerized) patient record. For over 40 years, the prospect of having all of the patient's medical information computerized and, thereby, easily accessed and evaluated by those who need to know, has eluded us. A primary barrier has been the lack of standards for recording and retaining data that permit exchange between a diverse set of computers and data systems. The time has come to sort this mess out and move ahead with computerization of patients' medical records. With proper safeguards, currently available, computerization would enable both patients and their doctors to instantly access information, regardless of where they are. The benefits in terms of emergency care in far-off places are obvious. Less dramatic, but much more common usage will be to facilitate exchange of information between specialists and other providers, which has great potential to reduce one of the common cause of errors: faulty communication.

Not only would a standardized electronic medical record vastly improve the efficiency and safety of patient care, the ability to easily and accurately collect large volumes of clinical data would vastly accelerate the development of evidence needed for the evidence based methods to be disseminated and adopted as wisely specified in Section 1185. In addition, with appropriate consent and confidentiality safeguards, the universal record could permit large population testing of new drugs within months of their release. Unsuspected side effects could be detected within months, instead of years at present, saving thousands of lives.

I recommend not only passage of section 1184, and Section 3, establishment of a Medical Information Technology Advisory Board, but also that Congress provide financial incentives, such as bonuses by CMS, for hospitals that implement computerized patient records.

Protection of voluntarily reported patient safety data

None of the recommendations from the IOM were as controversial as those for reporting of adverse events. Much of the controversy arose from misunderstandings about the nature of mandatory reporting. For many years, a number of states have had mandatory reporting systems in which hospitals (not doctors) are required to report particularly serious adverse events (not errors). The IOM recommended that all states implement such programs, and further recommended standardizing the types of events to be reported in order to facilitate aggregation of data for learning purposes. AHRQ commissioned the National Quality Forum (NQF) to develop such a list of serious reportable events, which it did and published last year.

The IOM also recommended that voluntary reporting of less serious events be encouraged. Reporting systems can advance patient safety in several ways. First, if incidents are promptly reported, it can serve as an "early warning system" to alert all providers of new hazards. The medication error reporting program (MERP) run by the US Pharmacopoeia (USP) and the Institute for Safe Medication Practices (ISMP) has performed this function for medication errors for years, as does the FDA

MedWatch program for adverse drug reactions. Second, by aggregating large numbers of reports from many institutions, a national reporting system can identify patterns of injury that are not obvious to those at the local level, particularly for rare events or those with unusual causes. Third, lessons learned by individual hospitals of new methods to prevent errors can be disseminated. Fourth, analysis can lead to recommendations for "best practices" for all to follow.

It is important to recognize that reporting alone does not improve safety. Reports must be analyzed and lead to recommendations for changes in care, and those changes must be implemented. Analysis of reports is an expensive enterprise, requiring a high level of expertise. It is far more costly than the data entry component of a reporting system, yet those costs have rarely been considered when proposals are made for a national system. For example, the ASRS run by NASA for aviation receives over 30,000 reports annually and costs approximately $70 per case. The annual number of preventable injuries in health care is estimated to be over 1 million. A successful national reporting system for health care conducted at a similar level of expert analysis as ASRS could cost as much as $70 million per year.

A more feasible option, which in fact is occurring, is the development of system-wide programs, such as that being developed by NASA for the VA, and specialty-based focused reporting programs, such as those developed by neonatal and adult intensivists. Similar programs could be developed by other health care systems and specialties.

No voluntary reporting system will be successful, however, unless reporting is safe. Fear of discovery with potential adverse legal consequences is a major inhibitor of reporting by hospitals and doctors in all states. Evidence from many sources, within and outside of medicine, as well as the accumulated experience of several decades, demonstrates that people will not report or discuss information that puts them at risk of adverse personal consequences. If we want this information in order to learn from our mistakes, we must make it safe for people to report. The proposed legislation wisely provides legal protection for information submitted voluntarily to patient safety improvement systems. This feature is crucial for the success of all voluntary reporting systems, public or private.

Unfortunately, in Section 1182 (d) (2) PERMISSIBLE DISCLOSURES, Disciplinary Proceedings, those protections are removed if the information is needed as part of a disciplinary procedure. That single clause nullifies all of the benefits of this section. No thinking doctor, nurse or hospital administrator will provide potentially incriminating information to anyone under these circumstances. They will not report. Nor should we expect them to. If this clause is retained, this legislation will have no impact on reporting. It will not change the status quo.

Nor is this type of disclosure necessary. Current regulations already mandate reporting of serious adverse events, including the results of investigations carried out by hospitals, in many states. Disciplinary proceedings, whether within the hospital or conducted by State Medical Boards, are also governed by detailed and tested rules that assure fair and full exploration of instances of suspected misconduct. State regulatory bodies have many legitimate methods for obtaining information. It is only the reports that leave the hospital that need protection. Much of the information is available in other places. The medical record is available, for example, and while the individual at risk cannot (rightfully, under our Constitution) be forced to testify against himself, other parties have both contractual and legal obligations to provide information. That is more than sufficient to meet disciplinary needs.

I strongly recommend that the Committee delete section 1182 (d) (2). If it remains, the so-called "protection" against discovery will be meaningless.

Chairman JOHNSON. Thank you very much, Dr. Leape. Dr. Wood?

STATEMENT OF MICHAEL B. WOOD, M.D., PRESIDENT AND CHIEF EXECUTIVE OFFICER, MAYO FOUNDATION, ROCHESTER, MINNESOTA, AND MEMBER, HEALTHCARE LEADERSHIP COUNCIL

Dr. WOOD. Madam Chairman, I appreciate this opportunity to speak with you today on a matter of utmost importance to all Americans, that is, the level of safety afforded to each and every patient who enters our health care system. This Committee is to be commended for the attention you are giving this vitally important issue.

I am President and Chief Executive Officer of the Mayo Foundation, based in Rochester, Minnesota. All of us at Mayo are proud of our institution's worldwide reputation for excellence in patient care, medical education, and medical research. We are devoted to innovation and constant improvement.

Today, I am testifying on behalf of my colleagues and counterparts who are members of the Healthcare Leadership Council (HLC). The Healthcare Leadership Council is a coalition of chief executives of the Nation's leading health care companies and organizations representing all sectors of health care, from hospitals to health plans, from pharmaceutical companies to medical device manufacturers. These members are committed to patient safety, quality care, and continuous improvement and innovation.

It is important to note that the health care industry is already taking numerous steps to reduce error rates and to continually increase the quality of care we provide for the patients. Many health care providers are reducing human error by upgrading systems technologies. At Mayo facilities, for example, we are moving toward a completely paperless environment, including the computerization of patient records for better access, clearer notations, and improved care.

Other Healthcare Leadership Council Member companies are also involved in increasing the use of computerized physician order entry, computerized on-floor pharmacies, and scanning bar codes at the patient's bedside to reduce the potential for medication errors.

As well, manufacturers are instituting dose-by-dose packaging, improving dosage and interaction instructions, and eliminating look-alike packages and product names, all measures well known to prevent drug-related accidents.

Thus, we are seeing the development of a strong public-private partnership to enhance patient safety. However, in addition to the innovations and improvements that are taking place, patients will be well served if Congress adopts measures, such as the bill that you have introduced, Madam Chairman, H.R. 4889, the Patient Safety Improvement Act of 2002. Legislation such as this will provide a valuable assist to health care providers in conducting the kind of information sharing essential to quality improvement.

In order to achieve widespread and continuous improvements in patient safety, there are three directions we must pursue. First, the health care industry must work together to develop standards that will encourage widespread use of information technology systems. You have strongly encouraged this, Madam Chairman, and you are absolutely right to do so. This is a priority of ours at Mayo Clinic because we know that modern information technology can make the patient record more complete, more accurate, and more accessible and reduce the possibility of errors.

Second, we believe that continued emphasis must be placed on voluntary reporting of medical errors and confidentiality protections to encourage sharing of information. To make our health system safer, health providers must be able to collect and analyze patient safety data. We need to avoid punitive measures and an increased exposure to litigation that would simply drive critically important information underground.

Your legislation, Madam Chairman, utilizes peer review protections in a very positive way to encourage the development and sharing of critical data and especially to bring near-misses out in the open for analysis and process improvements before they do harm.

In the discussions we have had thus far today, it is important to recognize that the major opportunity to prevent medical errors is to identify error-prone processes in health care. Voluntary non-punitive reporting brings these near-misses to light and, conversely, mandatory reporting will continue to drive the near-misses into the shadows.

Witness, for example, that in the Joint Commission on Accreditation of Healthcare Organizations (JCAHO) Sentinel Events Project we have seen reported 2,000 sentinel events in 5 years, whereas the MedMARx near-misses voluntary reporting system has brought forward 400,000 in 1 year, which represents the major opportunity we are seeing.

Finally, the third area that we need to address is that we must adopt safe practice standards that are evidence-based and have the flexibility to accommodate evolving science and new medical technologies. It will not serve patients well to use regulatory mandates to freeze practices in place today that could well be outdated in mere months.

In closing, I want to again commend this Committee for the energy and attention it is focusing on this important issue. Having a hearing like this is conducive to developing the culture of awareness to which I alluded earlier. I am confident that government and the health care industry can work together cooperatively and constructively to create an environment that encourages constant quality improvement. This is an important challenge affecting the lives and safety of every American patient and it is a challenge that we intend to meet.

Once again, thank you for the opportunity to share these views of the Healthcare Leadership Council.

[The prepared statement of Dr. Wood follows:]

Statement of Michael B. Wood, M.D., President and Chief Executive Officer, Mayo Foundation, Rochester, Minnesota, and Member, Healthcare Leadership Council

Madam Chairman, I appreciate this opportunity to speak with you today on a matter of utmost importance to all Americans, the level of safety afforded to each and every patient who enters our health care system. This committee is to be commended for the attention you are giving to this vitally-important issue.

I am President and Chief Executive Officer of the Mayo Foundation, based in Rochester, Minnesota. All of us at Mayo are proud of our institution's worldwide reputation for excellence in clinical practice, education and medical research. We are devoted to innovation and constant improvement B principles that we apply intensely to the area of patient safety.

Today, I am testifying on behalf of my colleagues and counterparts who are members of the Healthcare Leadership Council. The HLC is a coalition of chief executives of the nation's leading health care companies and organizations representing all sectors of health care. We meet on a regular basis to jointly develop policies, plans and programs to achieve our vision of a patient-centered 21st century health care system.

It is important that an organization like the HLC be centrally involved in a national discussion on the best ways to improve patient safety. No single health care sector can act in a vacuum in addressing this issue. Hospitals, medical device manufacturers, health plans, pharmaceutical companies, pharmacies, purchasing companies B all must work in consensus to achieve new advances in patient safety, and to ensure that those advances have widespread implementation.

The HLC is developing this consensus through its Chief Executive Task Force on Patient Safety. Through this task force, leaders from all sectors of health care are working cooperatively to elevate public confidence in patient safety. We are united behind a self-initiated protocol for addressing patient safety positively and responsibly.

It is important to note that the health care industry is already taking numerous steps to reduce error rates and to continually increase the quality of care we provide to patients. Many health care providers are reducing human error by upgrading systems technologies. At Mayo facilities, we are moving toward completely paperless environments, including the computerization of patient records for better access, clearer notations and improved care.

Other HLC member companies are involved in increased use of computerized physician order entry, computerized on-floor pharmacies, and scanning barcodes at the patient's bedside to reduce the potential for medication errors. As well, manufacturers are instituting dose-by-dose packaging, improving dosage and interaction instructions, and eliminating look-alike packages and product names.

Many hospitals are voluntarily submitting error data to organizations like the Joint Commission on Accreditation of Health Organizations and U.S. Pharmacopia, where they receive helpful analysis and feedback on how to avoid similar errors in the future. These are just a few of the many examples of activities underway within a health care industry that is committed to error reduction and improved safety.

We are seeing the development of a strong public-private partnership to enhance patient safety. In addition to the innovations and improvements taking place in the public sector, patients will be well served if Congress adopts measures such as the bill you introduced, Madam Chairman, H.R. 4889, the "Patient Safety Improvement Act of 2002." Legislation such as this will provide a valuable assist to health care providers in conducting the kind of information sharing essential to quality improvement. The members of the Healthcare Leadership Council stand ready to work with you to see this approach become law.

In my testimony today, I would like to address three points that are absolutely critical if we are to significantly reduce medical errors and give all patients the confidence that they will receive care that is safe and of the highest quality. First, we must consider the critical role information technology will play in improving patient safety. Second, we need to emphasize the importance of confidentiality and voluntary reporting in the handling of errors, so that we can use the knowledge gained from medical errors to build better, safer health care systems. And, finally, we need to discuss the best methods for developing safe practice standards.

Information Technology Standards

As I mentioned previously, the Mayo Clinic is moving toward a completely paperless environment, including paperless patient records. We have, in fact, completed this process at our Jacksonville, Florida facility. We are doing this because we believe the use of information technology can help ensure the completeness of the patient record, make it more accessible for all health professionals involved in the patient's care, and reduce the possibility of errors. With an electronic record, there is greater assurance that information concerning diagnoses, medication, imminent surgeries and the like is accurate and complete.

There is no question that information technology has enormous potential to help us reduce the possibility of errors, and health care organizations, lawmakers and other policy officials should support the automation of patient safety systems to the greatest extent possible. The Institute of Medicine is urging a new generation of patient safety systems that are automated, information system-based and driven by sound technologies. Certainly, a voluntary health information infrastructure should be encouraged and facilitated as rapidly and as broadly as possible.

There are challenges in this area for which we must develop solutions. Some hospitals, facing budget constraints, are reluctant to purchase these technologies because of concerns that they cannot be integrated with their current IT systems, or because they fear newer, better systems could soon be released which would make their major technology investments obsolete.

The health care industry must work together to develop standards that will encourage widespread usage of information technology systems. HLC is a founding member of the National Association of Health Information Technology. Madam Chairman, you called upon the industry to act proactively in this area, saying that "if you don't, we will." We take that charge very seriously and, with the creation of NAHIT, we intend to work toward standards that will maximize the advantages technology can bring in reducing medical errors. We also intend to work closely with the medical information technology board that H.R. 4889 would create to ensure the development and dissemination of best practices in medical information technology.

Confidentiality and Voluntary Reporting

Our success in improving patient safety will be largely dependent upon the environment we create for handling medical errors and mining the vitally-important knowledge that can be gained from those occurrences. We must have a culture of awareness, not a culture of blame.

Health care providers must be able to collect and analyze patient safety data, and to use that information to develop better, safer systems. There is a mutual exclusivity between laws that perpetuate litigation and our efforts to transform adverse events and "near mises" into permanent and pervasive system improvements. To put it simply, an increased likelihood of lawsuits will drive this critically-important information underground. The same philosophy applies to the issue of voluntary versus mandatory reporting. We must use positive incentives to encourage hospitals and providers to swiftly report health care delivery problems. Mandatory reporting would be viewed as a punitive effort by the government to extract information from private entities B information that could then be used against them in costly litigation.

Current mandatory reporting programs have been less successful than their supporters envisioned. Compliance with these programs has been inconsistent, due to the punitive nature of the programs and ineffective use of the submitted data. Mandatory reporting requirements, and the increased likelihood of punitive results against health care professionals and organizations, has effectively suppressed error reporting and inhibited open discussion about medical errors.

Existing voluntary reporting systems, on the other hand, have been successful because of their strong focus on improving practitioner performance instead of punitive results. Examples of successful voluntary systems, such as those from the aviation and motor vehicle industries, show dramatic improvements in reporting levels, product design and personnel training. We can learn from these examples that quality improvement requires the design of systems focused on prevention of human error rather than on assigning blame.

Lawmakers must carefully consider any new laws or regulations that could actually do damage to the current health care system by making errors and "near misses" even harder to identify. Confidentiality protections should be instituted to protect organizations from the fear of litigation that would inhibit and prevent the sharing of information. We are pleased, Madam Chairman, to see such peer review protections included in your legislation. With this protection, hospitals will be encouraged to share information with organizations that can analyze it to determine common error patterns and recommend system improvements.

To improve patient safety nationwide, we must create this culture of awareness nationwide as well. Today, some states have strong peer review protections while others do not. These inconsistencies serve as barriers for any patient safety initiatives that involve institutions in multiple states. Moreover, information relating to patient safety and "near-misses" may run the risk of losing peer review protection when shared outside of an institution. This often creates a greater degree of liability exposure than many providers are willing to tolerate.

Safe Practice Standards

We would all agree that safe practice standards should be in effect to assure the highest quality of care for all patients, regardless of the physician or institution treating them. We must carefully consider, though, how to develop the most effective standards that will have widespread acceptance and the flexibility to accommodate new innovations in health care.

We believe that nationally-recognized safe practice standards should be developed only through analysis of conclusive data on broad, evidence-based effectiveness and feasibility. And these standards must consider evolving science. Additionally, we must recognize that not all health care institutions or patient populations are exactly alike and, therefore, health care organizations should be encouraged to adopt safe practice programs that are applicable to their unique specialties, patient populations and specific risk points.

Some have expressed the belief that government should develop and enforce universal standards of care. Rigid government regulations in this arena, we believe, would not serve the best interests of patients. Knowledge and innovation in health care is constantly evolving, constantly improving. The practices we freeze in place today with regulatory mandates could well be outdated in mere months.

It is vitally important that practice standards not stifle scientific innovations. If a set of safe practices were to become universally-required standards of care, they could effectively establish a ceiling for patient safety practices, and discourage further innovations for even safer practices. While one might argue that national practice standards could be periodically reviewed and updated, the well-known reality is that our current regulatory process does not accommodate the kind of rapid and substantial changes that new technologies can necessitate. There is also concern that government-enforced standards of care may not be feasible for all hospitals and health providers throughout the nation.

There is a commitment on the part of the health care industry to develop safe practice standards B standards that are meaningful, feasible and that will encourage, not stifle, future improvements. The Healthcare Leadership Council is an active member of the National Quality Forum, and we will continue to work extensively to develop workable standards to achieve the best in patient care.

In closing, I want to again commend this committee for the energy and attention it is focusing on this important issue. Having a hearing like this is conducive to developing the culture of awareness to which I alluded earlier. I am confident that government and the health care industry can work together cooperatively and constructively to create an environment that encourages constant quality improvement. This is an important challenge affecting the lives and safety of every American patient, and it is a challenge that we intend to meet. Once again, thank you for this opportunity to share the views of the Healthcare Leadership Council.

Chairman JOHNSON. Thank you very much, Dr. Wood. Mr. Segel?

STATEMENT OF KENNETH T. SEGEL, DIRECTOR, PITTSBURGH REGIONAL HEALTHCARE INITIATIVE, PITTSBURGH, PENNSYLVANIA

Mr. SEGEL. Chairman Johnson, Congressman Stark, and Members of the Subcommittee, thank you very much for the opportunity to testify on the Patient Safety Improvement Act of 2002.

As brief background to my comments, I want to provide an update on the patient safety activities of the Pittsburgh Regional Healthcare Initiative (PRHI), which I direct. The PRHI is a collaborative effort among all of Southwestern Pennsylvania's major stakeholders in health care. Our goal is to establish the world benchmark for patient outcomes by identifying and solving problems at the point where patients are cared for.

We have five major clinical improvement projects and two major patient safety projects. We take much of the inspiration for our efforts from Pittsburgh-based Alcoa, which under now-U.S. Department of the Treasury Secretary Paul O'Neill became the world's safest organization.

We now include 42 hospitals that are working collaboratively to eliminate medication errors and nosocomial, or health care acquired, infections. They are all using the same data reporting systems to share learning about these problems, including U.S. Pharmacopeia's MedMARx for medication errors and the Centers for Disease Control's National Nosocomial Infectious Surveillance system for infections. In this work, we have received invaluable assistance from critical Federal partners under Secretary Thompson's direction, including the Centers for Disease Control, the Agency for Health Care Research and Quality, and the Centers for Medicare and Medicaid Services.

We have seen early signs of progress, including drops in our first targeted type of infection, catheter-associated bloodstream infections, which have fallen by 22 percent in 1 year. We have also seen sharp increases in the number of medication errors reported in our community and a reduction in death following cardiac bypass surgery of 14 percent in 1 year. So, we are acting in our community to address the concerns identified by the Institute of Medicine and by our own community.

Despite that progress, however, our efforts continue to be slowed, sometimes dramatically, by the cautiousness of most hospitals and clinicians to share information about errors openly due to fear of suit. This fear continues to introduce torturous procedures and cautions into the process of error reporting, analysis, sharing of learning, and improvement. In that context, we believe this legislation would promote the more open, honest, and effective reporting and analysis of errors that medicine so desperately requires.

To be most useful to you, I want to use my final minutes to talk about some specific components of the bill, because our experience tells us that the devil really will be in the details in terms of how this legislation is interpreted by the health care legal community as well as the courts.

In terms of patient safety data that is covered, we were very encouraged to see that the legislation does not limit protection to patient safety data collected solely for the purpose of reporting to a . This is essential to reflect the real world of health care delivery and hospital processes. The inclusion of the word "solely" or an equivalent would impose the creation of parallel processes of error identification, analysis, and corrective action on institutions. They would be left with the present faulty patchwork of peer review law, which itself has its own cumbersome restrictions on what happens within institutions, as well as providing too little external support to deal with error reporting. It would lead to, we fear, less than enthusiastic and complete use of the reporting process contemplated here.

In this regard, we also strongly recommend that you make explicit that the bill's protections would apply to corrective actions taken by a provider internally in response to patient safety data, even before waiting for feedback from a . Again, this reflects operating reality and our shared goal for this bill, which is to have errors surfaced and resolved as close to real time as possible, and we do not want to make people wait to have to take action in terms of feedback coming back. The legislation's rules of construction seem to provide that protection, but we might even make it more explicit.

In terms of the definition of health care provider, we would urge you to expand that to include health insurers. They have rich data sets that can be sources of information and learning on errors that should be explicitly covered.

We strongly agree with the previous witnesses that the provisions on the interoperability of health care information technology systems be enacted. It is a critical step forward, with potentially incalculable gains for patient care.

Finally, on the issue of voluntary or mandatory reporting, this is a challenging public policy question. It is one that will be played out in Pennsylvania over the next several years as a new mandatory reporting requirement goes into place. I do want to suggest strongly, based on our own experience and our own interactions with the health care systems, that there needs to be a significant period of trust building with the health care community via a voluntary non-punitive error reporting system before Congress consider it necessary to enact mandatory reporting provisions.

If Congress proceeds with a mandatory emphasis right away, it will frame the issue in the traditional mode of regulatory compliance played between regulators and providers, and the providers have many quills in their arsenal. Within health care institutions, I can tell you it will leave implementation firmly in the hands of the conservative, cautious lawyers and risk managers that so influence hospital practice in these areas, not uniformly so, but significantly so, and an opportunity to redefine how we think and approach these issues by providing the protection and safety that people need to take action will have been lost.

So, we strongly support this bill and we hope that its essential protections can be enacted into law so that we can move forward expeditiously to identify and solve problems quickly.

[The prepared statement of Mr. Segel follows:]

Statement of Kenneth T. Segel, Director, Pittsburgh Regional Healthcare Initiative, Pittsburgh, Pennsylvania

Chairman Johnson, Congressman Stark and Members of the Subcommittee:

Thank you for your invitation to comment on H.R. 4889, the Patient Safety Improvement Act of 2002. It was an honor for Karen Wolk Feinstein, Ph.D., Chair of PRHI to testify before you on patient safety issues this spring, and we are honored to be asked to provide you with our perspective again today. Given the depth and sensitivity with which you have examined these issues, the importance of the legislation you have compiled is not a surprise.

As brief background to my comments, I want to provide an update on the patient safety activities of the Pittsburgh Regional Healthcare Initiative (PRHI).

PRHI is a collaborative effort among all of the region's major stakeholders in health care, including clinicians, hospitals, insurance plans, corporations and small-business purchasing alliances, labor, and even the Attorney General of Pennsylvania. Our goal is to establish the world benchmark for patient outcomes in Southwestern Pennsylvania, by identifying and solving problems "at the point where patients are cared for." We have five major clinical improvement projects, and two major patient safety projects. We take much of the inspiration for our efforts from Pittsburgh-based Alcoa, which under now-Treasury Secretary Paul O'Neill, became the world's safest organization.

PRHI now includes 42 hospitals working collaboratively to eliminate medication errors and nosocomial (healthcare acquired) infections. As part of that effort, participating hospitals are all using the same medication error (US Pharmacopeia's MedMARx) and nosocomial infection reporting systems (the Centers for Disease Control's NNIS). In this work, we have received invaluable assistance from critical federal partners, including the Centers for Disease Control, the Agency for Healthcare Research and Quality, and the Center for Medicare and Medicaid Services.

We have seen encouraging but early signs of progress, including drops in our first targeted type of infection—catheter associated blood stream infections in intensive care units—which have fallen by 28% in one year. We have also seen sharp increases in the number of medication errors reported. While Pittsburgh area hospitals constitute roughly 5% of the hospitals using MedMARx nationally, they contribute roughly 10% of the medication error reports. Of course this is encouraging news, because the vast majority of medication errors are unreported, and only by reporting can they be learned from and other errors prevented. Through our additional collaborative efforts to improve clinical outcomes for patients, we have seen a 14% drop in mortality following cardiac bypass operations in one year (between 1999 and 2000), and are the only region in Pennsylvania with a lower death rate than could be expected given the risk-level of our cardiac patients. 40 more cardiac bypass patients are alive today because of the work of our cardiac surgery community.

So, we are acting to address the concerns identified by the Institute of Medicine and our own community.

Despite progress, however, our efforts continue to be slowed dramatically by the cautiousness of most hospitals and clinicians to share information about errors openly due to fear of suit for even the discussion and analysis of errors. This introduces tortuous procedures and cautions into the process of error reporting, analysis, sharing of learning, and improvement as a result.

In that context, we believe H.R. 4889 would promote the more open, honest, and effective reporting, and analysis of errors that medicine desperately requires. You have modeled your efforts on other high-risk industries such as aviation and nuclear power where such approaches have proven to save lives. We hope your colleagues in Congress recognize the urgency of echoing these models in health care, where lives are being lost every day for lack of such a protected reporting and analysis structure.

To be most useful to you, I want to comment on a few critical aspects of the bill as presently structured, and suggest modifications that might strengthen it. As our experience "on the ground" has taught us, the devil is in the details of how the critical provisions of this legislation would be interpreted in the courts and by the healthcare legal community.

Patient Safety Data Covered (section 1181(e)(1)(a) and 1181(e)(1)(c))

1) We were very encouraged to see that your legislation does *not* limit protection to patient safety data collected *"solely"* for the purposes of reporting to a patient safety organization, such as other federal legislation has proposed. This is essential to reflect the "real world" of healthcare delivery and hospital processes. The inclusion of the word "solely" or an equivalent restriction would impose the creation of parallel processes of error identification, analysis and corrective action on institutions. They would be left with the present faulty patchwork of peer review law to "protect" any internal error reporting and patient safety improvements that were not initiated "solely" in relation to a patient safety organization. This would lead to less than enthusiastic and complete use of the patient safety organization reporting process. We urge you to stand firm for your "common sense" approach to this critical definition.

2) In this regard, we strongly recommend that you make explicit that the bill's protections would apply to corrective actions taken by a provider internally in response to patient safety data, even before waiting for feedback from a patient safety organization. Again, this reflects operating reality. The goal is to have errors surfaced and resolved as close to "real time" as possible. If providers are forced to wait for external direction and feedback from a PSO before taking any action on data they report in order to enjoy any legal protection regarding the corrective action having been taken, we would undermine the likely scale and impact of corrective steps.

This clarification is especially important given the requirements for independence of the PSOs.

Definition of Health Care Provider (1181(d))

3) We recommend that you expand the definition of covered entities to include health insurers. Because of their comprehensive data sets, insurers often have rich information about errors and error prevention efforts that should be available for learning under the protections of this act. Absent explicit inclusion of insurers as entities that can report and derive protection under the legislation, this source of knowledge will go untapped by the nation.

Interoperability of Health Care Information Technology Systems (1184)

4) We want to applaud this component of the legislation and urge you to take all steps within your power to see that such interoperability standards are established. The gains to quality and safety of health care, and efficiency of the healthcare delivery system would be truly enormous.

Voluntary or Mandatory Reporting

We understand that one of the issues under discussion is whether reporting by healthcare organizations under the proposed Act should be voluntary or mandatory. This is a challenging public policy question—one that will be played out in Pennsylvania over the next several years due to the passage of legislation requiring reporting of safety incidents within 24 hours of confirmation. But let us suggest that there should be years of trust-building with the healthcare community in a voluntary error-reporting system before Congress consider mandatory reporting provisions. If Congress proceeds with a mandatory requirement right away, it will frame the issue in the traditional mode of regulatory compliance played between regulators and providers, and within healthcare institutions will leave implementation firmly in the hands of the conservative, cautious lawyers that so influence hospital practice in these areas. An opportunity to redefine how we approach issues of healthcare performance will have been lost.

In that mode, we would encourage Congress to think boldly in terms of "carrots" instead of just sticks to encourage future reporting.

In conclusion, we applaud your leadership and sensitivity in moving this essential legislation. We believe that if its essential protections can be enacted into law, it can make a profound impact on the safety, quality and value of healthcare services in our community, and the United States.

Chairman JOHNSON. Thank you, Mr. Segel. Dr. Pardes?

STATEMENT OF HERBERT PARDES, M.D., PRESIDENT AND CHIEF EXECUTIVE OFFICER, NEW YORK-PRESBYTERIAN HEALTH CARE SYSTEM, NEW YORK, NEW YORK

Dr. PARDES. Thank you very much, Chairman Johnson, thank you for your leadership both in our own tri-State area and nationally, and thank you, too, Mrs. Thurman, for your leadership.

It is a wonderful opportunity to address this issue of very great seriousness and also to talk about a bill with which I think holds great promise to address that issue, the use of information technology to prevent medical errors.

I am Herbert Pardes. I am a physician and President and Chief Executive Officer of New York-Presbyterian. We are the largest hospital system in New York State. We also have hospitals in Connecticut, New Jersey, and constitute one of the most comprehensive health care institutions in the world. We combined with New York Weill Cornell Medical Center and Columbia Presbyterian, and have two academic affiliates, the Weill Medical College of Cornell University and Columbia University College of Physicians and Surgeons.

Our system has some 51 acute care facilities, hospital facilities, residential health care facilities, and specialty institutions, more than 13,000 affiliated doctors, over 40,000 employees, and annually, over 400,000 inpatient discharges and 3.3 million outpatient visits, providing health care to some 5.5 million patients, some 22 percent of the Greater New York metropolitan region. We are placing a heavy focus, as some of my colleagues articulated, on health care quality and also patient services.

I wanted to focus particularly on the interoperability provisions of H.R. 4889 and I want to acknowledge the extraordinary work of Members of this House in the area of using information technology to protect patient health. First, Mrs. Johnson, who by introducing this bill has advanced the cause of safety to a new level. This bill is a quantum leap in solving the medical errors problems with tools that have not been used effectively in the past and needed someone of vision to stand by it.

Mr. Houghton of New York and Mrs. Thurman of Florida, your bill, H.R. 3292, the Medical Errors Reduction Act of 2001, paved the way for technology to be applied to patient safety. Your leadership has been central in this field.

Mr. Rangel, too, of New York, has understood and supported the notion that a new solution based on technology must be applied to health care for us to solve the old problems that have bedeviled us.

So, thank you all for your leadership. Thank you, too, Mr. Stark, for your leadership and concern about the needs of patients and the best interests of health care.

Patients suffer for lack of standards that would allow computer systems to exchange and process information across different vendor and specialty platforms. The lack of standards has been a huge barrier to the wise and widespread use of technology to prevent medical errors. In the vast majority of health care settings, a great deal of disparate information is collected on a patient, but the information is not presented to a clinician in a single computer screen. So, the data is only coordinated for the care of that patient when a clinician reviews it, usually when it is brought together on paper. If a result does not make it to the paper record, the clinician often is not aware of it when she makes her care decisions.

We feel there should be one computerized view of this information. Without adequate investment in elaborate interface technologies, different vendor systems cannot share all of the information. Standards would help obviate that need. Without standards, hospitals can never be sure of their investment in new technology. Will the existing systems work with new ones? Will new systems block the purchase of yet other equipment from different vendors?

Hospitals do not have the capital to revisit major information technology purchases on a year-after-year basis. While American industry generally spends between 7 and 10 percent of its revenues on information technology, health care, with its marginal economics, spends less than 3 percent.

In its interoperability provisions, the bill wisely creates the Medical Information Technology Advisory Board, to ensure that producers and consumers of health information, as well as those who provide the tools for collecting, storing, and exchanging this information, are part of the development process. The legislation should seek to support the real world application of these information technology standards by testing them in real patient care settings.

H.R. 4889 actualizes the potential of information technology in health care. Through an inclusive process that calls upon the expertise of industry, academic medicine, community medicine, public health, and government, the formation of the Medical Information Technology Advisory Board, which is thereby suggested or put forth, is necessary so interoperability solutions can be found that are applicable in the greatest number of health care settings, whether government or private.

Those who use information technology and those who manufacture it must be aligned from the beginning to design the right solutions. We have seen too often in the past how good technology fails because what has been designed for one environment does not necessarily translate into another. For example, excellent systems for administrative data exchange do not necessarily translate well for clinical care.

This bill coalesces those who produce health care data, those who consume it, and those who make the technology of storage and exchange around a single effort. There is one step, however, that is at least as important which is yet to be included in the legislation. H.R. 4889 needs to recognize that what happens at a theoretical level may not translate well into an operational environment, particularly in a field as complex as health care. For the vision of H.R. 4889 to be realized, we believe it is critical that demonstration projects to test the efficacy, use ability and scalability of information technology standards be conducted.

Scalability is a key determinant of success. A technology that appears to be a great idea in the inventor's garage and works beautifully in a dozen physicians' offices can fail when it has to care for millions of patients. Medicare and Medicaid's patients are found in every setting in America, large inner cities, sparse rural counties, suburban tracts, and local neighborhoods, so standards must be tested in a diversity of settings to ensure they will work wherever these patients and all Americans receive their care.

I urge you to add that support for demonstration projects to the legislation and I congratulate you again for this far-sighted solution. Most of all, I thank you for acting to solve what we feel is a most knotty problem, not with yesterday's thinking, but with tomorrow's technology, today's resolve, and a commitment to do something concrete and necessary for the best health interests of the American people. Thank you.

[The prepared statement of Dr. Pardes follows:]

Statement of Herbert Pardes, M.D., President and Chief Executive Officer, New York-Presbyterian Health Care System, New York, New York

Summary

- New York-Presbyterian Hospital is one of the nation's largest academic medical centers and is a center of excellence in the use of information technology (IT).
- IT in the clinical setting can reduce medical errors and increase quality of care through a wise national investment policy. The Computer-based Patient Record (CPR) is at the center of a technology strategy that would reduce errors. A complete CPR is impossible without standards for interoperability in healthcare IT.
- Hospitals are functioning at or below margin and are hard pressed to pursue the necessary investments to establish appropriate systems.
- Two major steps are needed: a standard setting process to allow interoperability among diverse systems from different vendors; and federal reimbursement. Academic medical centers have the expertise and neutrality to lead this process in collaboration with industry and government.
- The interoperability provisions of H.R. 4889 advance the right approach. They call for the formation of a board of experts from every effected constituency to recognize existing standards and develop or validate new standards. However, another step is also needed. Congress needs to allow for the demonstration projects that will assure the efficacy, usability and scalability of standards. As technology is developed for millions of patients rather than thousands, or even tens of thousands, scalability becomes a major stumbling block.

New York Presbyterian Hospital

New York-Presbyterian Hospital (NYP) is the largest hospital system in New York State and one of the most comprehensive healthcare institutions in the world. NYP represents a combination of two of the world's greatest medical resources, New York Weill Cornell Medical Center and Columbia Presbyterian Medical Center with their academic affiliates, the Weill Medical College of Cornell University and Columbia University College of Physicians & Surgeons. The NYP Health Care System (HCS) has a total of 51 acute care hospital facilities, residential health care facilities and specialty institutions, more than 13,000 affiliated doctors, over 40,000 employees, and annually over 400,000 inpatient discharges and 3.3 million outpatient visits providing healthcare to 5.5 million patients—22 percent of the greater New York metropolitan region. The Hospital and its affiliated institutions and medical schools are engaged in a large number of medical research projects and receive about $300 million in research funding annually.

NYP is the home of the Columbia University Department of Medical Informatics, which traces it roots to a 1981 National Library of Medicine (NLM) Integrated Academic Information Management System (IAIMS) initiative. The planning and prototype phases of that initiative led to the creation of the Center for Medical Informatics in 1987. In 1994, Columbia University made the Center a full-fledged department in the health sciences campus, with the same rights and responsibilities as other departments such as Medicine and Surgery.

Since the beginning, the Department's focus has been on research, teaching, and service. A phase III IAIMS grant and an IBM contract funded the development of the next generation Clinical Information System (CIS). CIS has served as the Department's living laboratory for medical informatics research, as a training ground for new informatics researchers, and as New York-Presbyterian Hospital's clinical system. The system is used by 95% of attending physicians and essentially all residents and fellows. It currently has 4000 unique users per month, and there are 2 million patients in the database.

Information Technology and Medical Errors

Computers have great promise in healthcare as tools for monitoring patient care to the most minute detail. According to the IOM, "The majority of medical errors do not result from individual recklessness but from basic flaws in the way the health system is organized—illegible writing in medical records has resulted in administration of a drug for which the patient has a known allergy—And the health care system itself is evolving so quickly that it often lacks coordination. For example, when a patient is treated by several practitioners, they often do not have complete information about the medicines prescribed or the patient's illnesses." In short, even highly competent physicians can be stymied by a system that makes timely access to accurate and legible information difficult.

Clinicians are very good at giving care. Information systems are very good at process. The errors described in the IOM report were seldom errors of judgment; they were mistakes in process. The man who had the wrong leg amputated; the woman who died from an overdose of chemotherapy; the child with the fatal allergy to anesthesia—if only the clinicians had been aware of that one missing vital piece of information, they would have known the right thing to do. In many industries, computers track such crucial information.

If all pertinent patient information were made rapidly and seamlessly available to doctors when they needed it, clinicians who are trained to use their judgment based on the available facts would be in a better position to make optimal decisions. Does the patient have an allergy to anesthesia? The system would automatically alert the anesthesiologist if an inappropriate drug is prescribed. On which breast does the mammography report identify a tumor? The system automatically generates a diagram on the computer's display to verify the location. Does the clinician administer an excessive dosage of medicine because she has misread the prescription? The system compares the dosage with information about the patient's condition and alerts the clinician when the dosage is out of range.

And thanks to the World Wide Web, the benefits of this technology are not limited to large academic medical centers. We have recently seen the introduction of technologies that can monitor patients at great distances over the Web. From the home or in other settings, patient data are analyzed before being passed on to clinicians, alerting them to changes that need attention and storing information for future reference.

One branch of medical informatics, the science underlying the development of information systems to improve health care and other areas of biomedicine, is called automated medical decision support. It has been studied for more than 20 years at leading institutions across the nation. In fact, the standard computer language for generating computer-based medical warnings and reminders is the Arden Syntax, developed in part by researchers at Columbia University's Department of Medical Informatics located at the New York-Presbyterian Hospital.

Yet, developing an integrated technology that meets all the needs of American health care will require research and development support. Transferring the technology to hospitals most in need will require additional funding support. Leading health care institutions have the expertise to develop these Clinical Information Systems, but not the funding.

A wise national policy for healthcare Information Technology (IT) should target resources and expertise to increase the application of IT to reduce medical errors and improve health care quality. The Institute of Medicine suggests that at least 44,000 patients, and as many as 98,000, die each year as a result of medical errors. Data on medication errors show that 2.8 percent of all hospitalized patients experience a preventable adverse drug event, resulting in increased morbidity and mortality as well as significant added cost to the healthcare system. The cost of preventable medication errors alone is estimated at $2 billion annually. Emerging technologies to reduce medication errors at the stage of both ordering and administration hold significant promise, particularly if they are able to coordinate all information from the patient's medical record. Technologies such as the Computer-based Patient Record (CPR) and secure Web-based communication with patients can enhance the coordination of care, support implementation of evidence-based practice and engage patients more fully as partners in their medical treatment. It makes sense to focus efforts on the CPR, which lies at the center of a comprehensive hospital IT system, rather than on any single element of the system. For example, a stand-alone Computerized Physician Order Entry system (CPOE) will not attain the Institute of Medicine's goal of a 50 percent reduction in preventable medical errors by 2005, according to the Stamford, Connecticut.-based Gartner Group's top ten list of IT issues confronting healthcare professionals. A CPOE system that is part of a CPR system linked to clinical alerts and decision support will be the means to secure that objective.

In fact, a broad-based national IT policy would address some of the most difficult problems in medicine in addition to preventing medical errors, including epidemiological data tracking to fight bioterrorism. It would ensure that patients receive the best care no matter where they live or travel. It would take advantage of the great global infrastructure—the Internet—and so be broadly available. It would incentivise industry—insurers, systems manufacturers and software companies—to participate in standards development.

Barriers to Bringing IT to Hospitals

Health care lags behind almost every other major industry segment in investment in Information Technology. Average IT spending per employee per year among all U.S. industries is about $6,900 per year. The banking segment spends almost $15,000 per employee on IT. The insurance industry spends more than $13,000 per employee and telecommunications clocks-in at more than $11,000 per employee. Health care invests only about $3,000 per employee per year on IT. Another way of casting this is that other industries spend from 7–10% of revenues on IT; healthcare is below 3%.

Yet Clinical Information Services can vastly improve the quality of health care with long-term benefits for overall costs. And it would be centered on the concept of the computerized patient record (CPR).

A computerized patient record would carry a patient's entire medical history and related information in a secure, privacy-protecting, Web-accessible database. There are three barriers to implementation of a national health information system policy.

- There is no standard platform technology or terminology for the CPR as there is for business and other applications;
- There is insufficient investment and financial incentive, by the government and the private sector; and
- There is insufficient leadership

The issue of standards, in particular, has been a huge barrier to the wise and widespread use of technology to prevent medical errors. In the vast majority of healthcare settings, a great deal of disparate information is collected on a patient but that information is not presented to a clinician on a single computer screen. Thus, the data is only coordinated for the care of that patient when a clinician reviews it, usually when it is brought together on paper. If a result doesn't make it to the paper record at the right time, the clinician will not be aware of it when she makes care decisions. Thus, there needs to be one computerized view of this information. This requires a large investment in elaborate interface technologies because different vendor systems can't automatically share all of the information with each other. Standards would obviate that need. Without standards, hospitals can never be sure of their investment in new technology. With standards, hospitals will be encouraged to invest in IT, knowing they will have a stable platform.

The solutions to these problems are within grasp. The Federal Government has a clearly definable role in creating solutions that will deliver to Americans the error-reduction promise of the CPR without being intrusive to care providers or the industries that support them.

These things must be done for an effective National Health Information System Policy to be accepted by health care providers, insurers and CIS manufacturers.

- Before standards that support interoperability can be promulgated or driven by market demand, they must be developed. There is room for much flexibility in such formats, as described in the IOM study For the Record. Standard setting efforts have been successful in creating protocols for transmitting health data. One example is Health Level 7 (HL–7), a protocol for transmitting health information that provides a solution to one of the many issues in interoperability of healthcare IT. HL–7 was supported by academic medical institutions for years in the face of industry skepticism. As more institutions adopted HL–7, the industry realized the advantage of being able to design to a standard and embraced it most profitably. The most important thing is to be able to securely share patient information among different caregivers and researchers. The Government should support research and development for standards by credible institutions through a demonstration process led by centers of excellence in academic medicine, with full collaboration by industry.

- CPR standards must aid hospitals in complying with HIPAA, the Health Information Portability and Accountability Act. HIPAA rightly mandates extreme care of confidential patient data. But its enactment has been stymied by a hodgepodge of competing interests and its implementation promises to be one of the largest unfunded mandates ever levied on the health care industry. A wise national health information system policy will create standards for easier, more affordable compliance.
- Medicare and Medicaid should include incentives for hospitals to comply with the standards of the National Health Information System Policy, and provide disincentives for noncompliance. It's cheaper to process an electronic transaction than a paper one—that's why banks used to reward customers to use ATMs instead of tellers. The Center for Medicare and Medicaid Services (CMS) has, in the past, viewed technology as a cost-center rather than an investment. Yet a CPR can reduce difficulty in a variety of reporting and compliance areas. Medicare can reap the same benefits from technology that private sector industries have, increasing productivity and quality through the strategic use of ***IT***. The Information Technology Association of America projects that an industry-wide investment in ***IT*** of $18.1 billion would yield gross savings of greater than $120 billion dollars for the healthcare industry over a six-year period. But unlike other industries, healthcare providers do not have the profit margins to invest for the future in this area.
- The Federal Government should provide funding to help hospitals invest in IT. Hospitals and academic medical centers are at the center of an integrated health IT system and will be among the greatest users of the technology. But they cannot alone shoulder the cost of developing a system that must be able to serve patients, doctors, government agencies and insurers. Clearly there is justification for a national investment in the development of such a system. In fact, a nationally functional system will only be built collaboratively. The system will be potentially useful for those areas of increasing shortage in health care providers—rural areas and the inner city. Support is given in a variety of underserved locales for aspects of care.

The Patient Safety Improvement Act Of 2002

H.R. 4889, The Patient Safety Improvement Act Of 2002, contains provisions on interoperability of healthcare IT that will allow information technology to fulfill its promise in the area of patient safety. I want to acknowledge the extraordinary work of several Members of the House in the area of using IT to protect patient health. First Chairwoman Johnson, who by introducing this bill has advanced the cause of safety to a new level. This bill is a quantum leap in solving the medical errors problem with tools that have not been used effectively in the past and needed someone of vision to champion it. Mr. Houghton of New York and Ms. Thurman of Florida, your bill H.R. 3292, the Medication Errors Reduction Act of 2001, paved the way for technology to be applied to patient safety. Your leadership has been *sine qua non* in this field. Mr. Rangel of New York has long understood that a new solution based on technology must be applied to healthcare for us to solve the old problems that have bedeviled us. Thank you also for your leadership and support of the interoperability provisions.

How does H.R. 4889 actualize the potential of IT in healthcare? The bill establishes an inclusive process that calls upon the expertise of industry, academic medicine, community medicine, public health and government. The formation of the Medical Information Technology Advisory Board (MITAB) is necessary so that interoperability solutions can be found that are applicable in the greatest number of healthcare settings, whether government or private. Those who use IT and those who manufacture it must be aligned from the beginning to design the right solutions. We have seen too often in the past how good technology fails because what has been designed for one environment does not translate to another. For example, excellent systems for administrative data exchange do not translate well for clinical care. The MITAB section of the bill would bring together those who produce healthcare data, those who consume it and those who make the media of storage and exchange around a single effort.

However, there is a step that is at least as important, which has yet to be included in this legislation. H.R. 4889 needs to recognize that what happens at a theoretical level may not translate well into an operational environment, particularly in a field as complex as healthcare. For the vision of H.R. 4889 to be realized, it is critical that demonstration projects to test the efficacy, usability and scalability of IT standards be conducted. Scalability is a key determinant of success. A technology that appears to be a great idea in the inventor's garage, and works beautifully in a dozen physician offices, can fail when it has to care for millions of patients. Medicare and Medicaid's patients are found in every setting in America, large inner cities, sparse rural counties, suburban tracts and local neighborhoods. So standards must be tested in a diversity of settings to ensure they will work wherever these patients, and all Americans, receive their care.

Congress has an opportunity rarely presented in history. It can instigate a paradigm shift by seizing today's revolutionary technology, and it can save lives by putting it in the hands of the nation's healers. It is time to convene the best minds in this field and develop the standards for technology that will be indispensable to our future health. Academic medical centers can collectively take the lead in developing the technology for patient and clinician needs, and billing and compliance requirements. But they must be part of a vigorous partnership with the government, physician organizations, insurers and corporations—all of which will benefit from a true national IT system.

Chairman JOHNSON. Thank you very much, Dr. Pardes. Ms. Rosenthal?

STATEMENT OF JILL ROSENTHAL, MPH, PROJECT MANAGER, NATIONAL ACADEMY FOR STATE HEALTH POLICY, PORTLAND, MAINE

Ms. ROSENTHAL. Thank you, Chairwoman Johnson, Congressman Stark, and Members of the Committee. My name is Jill Rosenthal and I am with the National Academy for State Health Policy, a nonpartisan, nonprofit public policy research organization that works with State governments to help them achieve excellence in health care policy and practice. Our organization has been working with the Institute of Medicine and States on the issue of patient safety since 1999.

Among the recommendations outlined in the IOM report, "To Err Is Human," is the call for two types of reporting systems, each designed to address a specific concern, mandatory reporting as part of a public system for holding health care organizations accountable for performance, and voluntary reporting to complement mandatory reporting by detecting system weaknesses before serious harm occurs. The IOM made clear there is the need for both mandatory public reporting and voluntary, confidential reporting.

As the IOM envisioned, a nationwide mandatory reporting system would be established by building on current State systems with funding provided to States for this purpose. States would be given this role because they are on the front line in protecting the public's health. States have the unique role and legal responsibility to license and provide oversight of health care facilities and professionals. The public looks to State government to ensure that the health care system takes measures to ensure care is safe.

Although States have struggled with lack of resources to implement reporting systems, they are embracing the challenge. Twenty

States have created mandatory reporting systems. More States are considering them and others would follow if resources were available.

According to State officials, mandatory systems play a vital role in facility oversight and provide a window into facility patient safety practices. In addition to investigating individual events and ensuring corrective action, many States share reported information with professional licensure boards when professional standards may have been violated and issue patient safety alerts and newsletters to help facilities improve safe practices. Unfortunately, this bill will likely interfere with States' capacity to meet their obligations.

Here is where the bill creates problems. The bill does not recognize the importance of separate reporting systems for accountability and learning. Without a mandatory system that provides accountability, there will be no check and balance and Congress and the public will have no way to know that voluntary reporting is reducing serious medical errors.

The bill does not distinguish between the purpose of collecting information about medical errors that result in serious harm and those that result in minimal harm. Voluntary systems are intended for events that cause minimal harm. Events that cause serious harm are intended for mandatory systems because these types of events may indicate serious system weaknesses. However, the bill defines patient safety so broadly that it applies to all events. As a result, the bill creates an additional burden on providers who may have to report the same events to two systems.

The bill does not recognize or support the State's role in ensuring accountability through mandatory systems. The bill could have a chilling effect on State efforts to collect data for the purposes of accountability. If duplication exists, providers are unlikely to support two separate reporting mechanisms and will likely lobby against State efforts to create mandatory systems, even though they have a different scope, purpose, and function. The bill authorizes funding for voluntary reporting but does not address the IOM recommendation to fund State-based mandatory systems.

The bill's confidentiality provisions may conflict with State reporting system provisions. The bill requires data reported to Patient Safety Organizations to be confidential and privileged. However, the IOM report recommended that analysis of individual serious events be made available to the public as part of a system of accountability. Since the bill requires reporting of all types of events, all events would fall under strict confidentiality protections.

In a later study, the IOM called for the health systems to be accountable to the public, to do their work openly, to make their results known to the public and to build trust through disclosure, even of the system's own problems. According to the IOM, a transparent health care system will improve trust and be more patient-centered and safer because patients would have information to make informed decisions about their care.

There are opportunities to improve the bill to meet the IOM's intent and eliminate some of the problems for States. One, clarify the scope, purpose, and function of voluntary reporting as separate from and complementary to State-based mandatory systems.

Two, recognize that State-based mandatory systems focus on cases that cause serious harm and may make information known to the public. Events that cause serious harm, death, and criminal events should not be given legal protection under a voluntary system.

Three, balance funding for improving national voluntary reporting with funding for State-based mandatory systems.

In closing, State and Federal Government need to represent consumers and assure them that the health care system is being held accountable for safety. A public reporting system that provides both a check and balance and public information is needed, as is a voluntary system for quality improvement. Without both, we cannot realize the IOM's goals and we fail to provide needed public accountability for patient safety. Thank you.

[The prepared statement of Ms. Rosenthal follows:]

Statement of Jill Rosenthal, MPH, Project Manager, National Academy for State Health Policy, Portland, Maine

Chairman Johnson, Congressman Stark and distinguished Members of the Committee:

My name is Jill Rosenthal and I am a project manager for the National Academy for State Health Policy, a non-partisan, non-profit public policy research organization that works with state governments to help them achieve excellence in their health care policy and practice.

Our organization has been working with the Institute of Medicine and states on the issue of patient safety since 1999. We have provided policy analysis, training, and technical assistance to states as they have attempted to address the Institute of Medicine's recommendations.

Among the recommendations outlined in the Institute of Medicine report *To Err is Human* is a call for two types of reporting systems, each designed to address a specific concern. Mandatory reporting was intended for events that cause serious harm or death, as part of a public system for holding health care organizations accountable for performance. Voluntary reporting was intended to complement mandatory reporting by detecting system weaknesses before the occurrence of serious harm. The Institute of Medicine made clear that there is a need for both mandatory, public reporting systems and voluntary, confidential reporting systems.

As envisioned by the Institute of Medicine, a nationwide mandatory reporting system should be established by building on current state systems. The IOM recommended that funding be provided to states for this purpose.

States are the appropriate entities to take on this role because they are on the front line in protecting the public's health. States have the unique role and legal responsibility to license and provide oversight of health care facilities and professionals. The public looks to state government to ensure that the healthcare system takes necessary measures to ensure care is safe.

Although states have struggled with a lack of resources to implement reporting systems, they are embracing the challenge. Today 20 states have created mandatory reporting systems. More states are considering enacting systems and others would follow if resources were available.

According to state officials, mandatory reporting systems play a vital role in hospital oversight by providing a window into hospital patient safety practices and developing more complete facility profiles. In addition to investigating individual events and ensuring corrective action, many states share reported information with professional licensure boards when professional standards may have been violated, and they issue safety alerts and newsletters to help facilities improve safe practices.

Examples:

- Colorado shares copies of some incident reports with professional licensing boards, the attorney general's office, and other relevant state agencies.
- Tennessee reviews corrective action plans while investigating complaints and during annual surveys to ensure that facilities have carried out their plans.
- In Kansas, surveyors are given a summary of all adverse findings for each facility. During surveys they examine facility risk management and assure

that corrective actions have been implemented and if additional problems are noted, that further corrective actions are taken.

- Massachusetts provides data to the Massachusetts Coalition for the Prevention of Medical Errors to determine approaches for alerting and informing facilities about the risk of errors and practices for addressing identified problems.
- New York's system includes a report generation function that allows facilities to track and trend their own incidents and to compare their performance against peer facilities, within their regions, and statewide.

States continually strive to improve their systems. We are currently working with states and the National Quality Forum to compare state lists of types of events with the National Quality Forum's (NQF) list of Serious Reportable Events in order to help states develop a standardized list of clearly defined events that can be easily implemented and that allows room for state flexibility.

Unfortunately, the bill before you will likely interfere with states' capacity to meet their obligations.

Here's where this bill creates problems:

The bill does not recognize the importance of establishing separate reporting systems for accountability and learning.

Without a mandatory system that provides accountability, there will be no check and balance and Congress and the public will have no mechanism to know that voluntary reporting is working to reduce serious medical errors.

The bill does not distinguish between the purpose of collecting information about medical errors that result in serious harm and those that result in minimal or no harm.

Voluntary reporting systems are intended to collect information about events that cause minimal or no patient harm. Events that cause serious harm or death are intended for mandatory systems because these types of events may indicate serious system weaknesses. However, "patient safety data" is so broadly defined in the bill that it applies to all types of events. As a result, the bill creates an additional burden on providers who may be required to report the same events to both state-based mandatory systems and the national voluntary system.

The bill does not recognize or support the states' role of ensuring accountability through mandatory reporting systems.

The bill could have a chilling effect on state efforts to collect data for purposes of accountability. If duplication exists, providers will be unlikely to support two separate reporting mechanisms and will likely lobby against state efforts to create mandatory reporting systems even though they have a different scope, purpose, and function than voluntary systems. The bill authorizes funding for the voluntary system but does not address the IOM recommendation to fund state-based mandatory systems.

The bill's confidentiality provisions may conflict with state reporting system provisions.

The bill requires data reported to patient safety organizations to be confidential and privileged. However, the IOM recommended that analyses of individual serious event reports should be made available to the public as part of a public system of accountability. Since the bill requires reporting of serious events in addition to those that cause minimal harm, all events would fall under strict confidentiality protections.

In a later study, the IOM called for health systems to be accountable to the public; to do their work openly; to make their results known to the public and professionals; and to build trust through disclosure, even of the systems' own problems. According to the IOM, a transparent health care system will improve trust, be more patient-centered, and safer, because patients would have information to make informed decisions about their care. Some organizations, such as the Veteran's Administration, have increased transparency already. The IOM points out that although many providers fear increased transparency could increase liability, some evidence shows that open disclosure of errors may *decrease* the likelihood of malpractice loss.

There are opportunities to improve the bill that would meet IOM's intent and eliminate some of the problems for states:

1. Clarify the scope, purpose, and function of voluntary reporting systems as separate and distinct from, and complementary to, state-based mandatory reporting systems. This would reduce duplication and confusion and lay the groundwork to address IOM recommendations. Confidential, voluntary

reporting systems should not preempt state public mandatory systems that collect information about events that cause death or serious harm in the 20 states with existing systems or in states that have yet to develop mandatory systems.

2. Recognize the role of state-based mandatory reporting systems as identified in the IOM report: to collect information on specific cases that cause serious harm or death for the purpose of accountability and to collect information that may become known to the public. Certain events, such as those that cause serious harm, death, and criminal events, should not inadvertently or intentionally be given legal protection under a voluntary system.
3. Balance funding for improvement of national voluntary reporting efforts with funding for state-based mandatory systems, as envisioned by the IOM report.

State and federal government need to represent consumers and assure them that the health care system is being held accountable for safety. A public reporting system that provides both a check and balance and public information is needed as is a voluntary system for quality improvement purposes. Without both, we cannot realize the Institute of Medicine's goals and we fail to provide needed public accountability for patient safety.

Background

The National Academy for State Health Policy

National Academy for State Health Policy is a non-partisan, non-profit public policy research organization that works with state governments to help them achieve excellence in their health care policy and practice. Since its inception in 1987, NASHP has provided state health policy leaders with access to timely, unbiased information on pressing healthcare issues. Because NASHP recognizes that responsibility for health care does not reside in a single state agency, department, or branch of government, it strives to foster productive interchange across all lines of authority. Each year, NASHP conducts policy analysis, provides training and technical assistance to states, and—through its publications, annual state health policy conference, media briefings, meetings, and website (www.nashp.org)—disseminates information designed to assist states in the development of practical, innovative solutions to complex health policy issues.

States with mandatory reporting

Twenty states have created mandatory reporting systems:

California	Nebraska	South Carolina
Colorado	Nevada	South Dakota
Connecticut	New Jersey	Tennessee
Florida	New York	Texas
Kansas	Ohio	Utah
Maine	Pennsylvania	Washington
Massachusetts	Rhode Island	

Information that states collect

Twenty state licensure and certification agencies require mandatory reporting of adverse events that occur in hospitals. Many of the reporting systems also collect information from ambulatory care centers and psychiatric hospitals. Some collect information from free-standing laboratories and outpatient mental health centers, nursing facilities, and other licensed facilities. For example, Colorado's reporting system requires reporting from general and acute care hospitals, ambulatory care centers, psychiatric hospitals, freestanding laboratories, freestanding outpatient mental health centers, nursing facilities, and other licensed facilities. Washington State's reporting system collects information from acute care hospitals only.

States identify and define reportable events in different ways although they require fairly similar data elements to be reported. Facility name, type of incident, and date of occurrence are required by all states. Most states also include patient identification, provider identification, description of the incident, person reporting the incident, action taken by facility, patient outcome/status, and notification of other parties (e.g. professional licensing boards). Some include identification of witnesses as well.

Standardizing elements within state reporting systems

One of the barriers that states face in implementing mandatory reporting systems is identifying an unambiguous and clearly defined list of reportable events. The IOM report called for a nationwide mandatory reporting system that provides for the collection of standardized information by state governments about adverse events that result in death or serious harm. The report urged Congress to designate the National Quality Forum (NQF) as the entity responsible for establishing and maintaining a core set of reporting standards to be used by the states. Through its Serious Reportable Events Project, the NQF used a voluntary consensus standards setting process to develop a set of serious, preventable adverse events that might form the basis for a national state-based event reporting system. Participants identified 27 serious adverse events that should be reported by all licensed healthcare facilities. As suggested in NQF's report, additional specification may need to be developed to ensure standardized data collection.

The National Academy for State Health Policy (NASHP) is working with the NQF and a group of states (SAFER: State Alliance for Error Reporting) to compare state lists of reportable events with the National Quality Forum's (NQF) list of Serious Reportable Events in order to determine areas of overlap and areas of difference. The result of the project will be a user's guide to help states develop a standardized list of clearly defined events that can be easily implemented and that allows room for state flexibility.

States considering mandatory reporting

Twelve bills dealing with some aspect of error reporting were introduced in seven states during the 2001 state legislative sessions. Of these, six bills (in MA, MD, NY, and PA) would require new types of mandatory reporting or would strengthen existing reporting requirements.

State protection and disclosure of data

The IOM recommended that errors that are identified through mandatory reporting systems and are part of a public system of accountability should *not* be protected from discovery. State investigations of individual incidents are available on request in most states. One state makes investigation reports available on the Internet. All reporting systems (8) reviewed during NASHP site visits protect patient specific information. Reporting system officials unanimously support protecting *patient* confidentiality.

Some states release aggregate data that does not identify the facilities or patients involved in the incidents (de-identified data). Data elements may include the most common injuries, the average number of incidents per facility, or the total number of incidents reported.

States less commonly provide aggregate data that identifies incidents by facility name, in part because underreporting leads to incomplete data, making it difficult to distinguish between facilities that *experience* more errors and those that *report* more errors because they are more compliant with reporting requirements. However, some states have considered releasing information on the number, type, frequency, and causes of errors by facility. To do so requires risk adjustments for age, relative illness, and other complex factors so that users can interpret the data accurately. States continue to struggle with developing risk adjustment methodologies that take into account relevant factors that may help explain the frequency of adverse events.

States may choose to change their approach to disclosure over time. Some may choose to release de-identified aggregate data in the early stages of the system's development and move toward facility-specific data as the system matures, reporting increases, and a risk-adjustment technique is identified.

<u>Examples:</u>

- Colorado's Internet site posts reported incidents and findings from state investigations. The site can be found at *www.cdphe.state.co.us/hf/hfd.asp*.
- Florida's statute makes reports confidential and not subject to discovery or admissible as evidence in civil lawsuits. Data cannot be shared with other state agencies. Aggregate data are available upon request but names of facilities and individuals are not available.
- Kansas prepares an annual report using aggregate data by facility size for the average number of incidents reviewed, the total number of reportable

events, and the total number of reportable events reported to each professional board.

- Massachusetts does not have any legal data protections for reported incidents. However, patient specific information and some peer review protected information may not be released. All information in the reporting system, including formal narrative reports, deficiency statements, and facility personnel interviewed during investigations, is available to the public upon request.
- In 2001, New York prepared its first annual report that identifies hospitals with reporting rates significantly below what is anticipated: *www.health.state.ny.us/nysdoh/commish/2001/nyports/nyports.htm.*
- Washington incident reports are subject to public disclosure but names of individuals are redacted.

How states use data

The overriding reason for mandatory reporting systems is to hold healthcare facilities accountable for preventable adverse events that result in serious injury or death. Accountability is achieved by investigating the event, providing expertise or information to help remedy the problem, and insuring that appropriate changes are made and sustained to avoid the problem in the future. Investigation may be made on-site by clinicians.

A secondary purpose of a mandatory reporting system may be to improve overall quality and patient safety across facilities. Over time as experience and expertise have grown, many state reporting systems have shared lessons learned from individual reporting incidents by aggregating data to identify trends. Some states issue patient safety alerts, distribute newsletters that highlight trends and best practices, and operate websites that can be used by facilities to compare their patient safety history to peer facilities.

To varying degrees, all states share information with professional medical, nursing, and pharmacy boards if reports indicate that a professional violation may have occurred.

Examples:

- Colorado has established an Occurrence Advisory Committee, composed of providers, consumers, and state representatives, to assist the state in making better use of reported data.
- Kansas publishes newsletters highlighting trends and describing practices to reduce repeat incidents in those areas.
- Massachusetts provides data to the Massachusetts Coalition for the Prevention of Medical Errors to determine approaches for alerting and informing facilities about the risk of errors and practices for addressing identified problems.
- New York's system includes a report generation function that allows facilities to track and trend their own incidents and to compare their performance against peer facilities, within their regions, and statewide.

Other state patient safety activities

- Public/private partnerships: Coalitions have diverse memberships, often including providers, government, insurers, health plans, consumers, and community stakeholders like major employers, labor unions, or teaching institutions. Stakeholders determine the mission, goals, objectives, and policies of the group. With the exception of peer review data, these groups share knowledge and resources with other interested parties in the community, including governmental bodies. They take actions to address specific problem areas, for example, medication errors, wrong site surgery, peer review protections for reported adverse events, and education of professionals about error prevention. Statewide public/private patient safety coalitions have been formed in twelve states: Arkansas, Colorado, Georgia, Maryland, Massachusetts, Michigan, Minnesota, Ohio, Pennsylvania, Tennessee, Virginia, and Wisconsin.
- Public purchasers: Public employee purchasers in Maine, Massachusetts, Minnesota, Washington, and Wisconsin have forged relationships with private providers to mobilize employer purchasing power to improve health care safety and give consumers information to make informed health care choices.
- State legislatures continue to increase their efforts to address patient safety.

SUMMARY OF STATE LEGISLATIVE ACTIVITY: 1999—2001*

	1999	2000	2001
No. of bills introduced	1[1]	34	61
No. of bills enacted	1	10[1]	12
No. of states introducing legislation	5[2]	14[3]	22[4]
Issues addressed by enacted legislation	whistleblower protections	whistleblower protections system-wide analysis; study commission; report to legislature reporting requirements improved safety through language access medication error reduction public disclosure of information	whistleblower protections system-wide analysis; access to data, study commission, report to legislature reporting requirements establishment of patient safety center required activities as condition of state licensure public disclosure of information

* most recent year available

NASHP documents on state activities related to patient safety

Sharon Conrow Comden and Jill Rosenthal, *Statewide Patient Safety Coalitions: A Status Report* (Portland, ME: National Academy for State Health Policy, May 2002).

Jill Rosenthal and Maureen Booth, *How Safe is Your Health Care? A Workbook for States Seeking to Build Accountability and Quality Improvement through Mandatory Reporting Systems* (Portland, ME: National Academy for State Health Policy, November 2001).

Jill Rosenthal, Maureen Booth, and Anne Barry, *Cost Implications of State Medical Error Reporting Programs: A Briefing Paper* (Portland, ME: National Academy for State Health Policy, May 2001).

Jill Rosenthal and Trish Riley, *Patient Safety and Medical Errors: A Road Map for State Action* (Portland, ME: National Academy for State Health Policy, March 2001).

Jill Rosenthal et al., *Current State Programs Addressing Medical Errors: An Analysis of Mandatory Reporting and Other Initiatives* (Portland, ME: National Academy for State Health Policy, January 2001).

Jill Rosenthal, Trish Riley, and Maureen Booth, *State Reporting of Medical Errors and Adverse Events: Results of a 50–State Survey* (Portland, ME: National Academy for State Health Policy, April 2000).

Chairman JOHNSON. Thank you, Ms. Rosenthal. Dr. Leape, I would like to return to your statement, at the end of your prepared remarks. You stated that section 1182(D) that allows disclosure for

[1] A Virginia bill was not enacted but was implemented in 2000 by request of the Speaker. That bill is counted as an enacted bill for 2000.
[2] HI, MA, NY, OK, and WA.
[3] CA, FL, HI, IL, MA, MN, MO, NJ, NY, PA, SD, VA, WA, and WV.
[4] CA, CT, FL, GA, IL, IN, IA, KY, ME, MD, MA, MI, MN, MO, NV, NH, NJ, NY, OR, PA, VA, and WV.

disciplinary proceedings and removes protections of that information needed as part of a disciplinary proceeding, would nullify all the benefits of the bill. Would you enlarge on that?

Dr. LEAPE. Yes, I would be pleased to. I think we ought to be clear that the bill provides protection for information that is shared from a hospital with a , and I think that is critically needed. Clearly, it does not mean that all the information is protected for any use whatsoever. For example, the information would include information that is in the medical record, the patient's diagnosis, what happened, all those things. Clearly, nobody has in mind that that should not be available.

For disciplinary procedures, all of that information is currently available. We have mechanisms now for disciplinary procedures, as we do for malpractice, which include the ability to examine witnesses, to take depositions, to examine the records in the hospital, and all of these, as I understand it, would not be impacted nor should be impacted by this legislation.

So, I do not think we need to remove that protection in order to achieve what we want in the way of appropriate disciplinary procedures. If that exclusion is there, then physicians and nurses will not report in the voluntary system. They will feel that they have, in effect, lost their peer review protection and I think it will literally set the process of voluntary reporting back.

Chairman JOHNSON. Thank you. I thought that was a very strong statement and we will—I will, at least—give it very careful consideration.

Dr. Wood, would you explain a little bit more thoroughly why the JCAHO process resulted in 2,000 events reported and why you think the MedMARx resulted in 400,000 in a year. That is an astounding difference in the amount of knowledge developed as a result of differently structured reporting systems. Now, what is the difference and why 2,000 versus 400,000?

Dr. WOOD. Madam Chairman, I think this relates back to the statement you made earlier in this hearing, that what we are really trying to do is to improve the error-prone care processes, in other words, systematic improvement.

What we see in the JCAHO sentinel events program is the reporting of the most egregious events, in other words, the events that result in death or harm. These are not the areas—this is not the focus of attention, to try to get to improvement in health care processes. The much greater opportunity are those things that are recognized as a potential accident that do not result in egregious harm to the patient. I think the statistics I quoted give some idea of the relative magnitude of those two opportunities.

That is why I think if we focus our attention through this bill on trying to draw out of the woodwork, if you will, the near misses, this will give us the best capacity to really get at and improve these processes, whereas if we continue to focus on those that are only the sentinel events, we will only see a small fraction and it will take us years and years to try to get at improved processes if those are the only ones that we are focusing on.

I think that is where the fundamental discussion about voluntary versus mandatory reporting comes out. The voluntary will help bring these near-misses out, whereas the mandatory will always drive those underground.

Chairman JOHNSON. A more concrete example, I think, in my life, is represented in a manufacturing portion of the country. For a long time, we focused on looking at our rate of perfection at the end of the manufacturing process and the amount of goods that you had to reject because they were not perfectly done. This was a very big issue, and we focused harder and harder and harder to try to bring down that error rate, if you will, at the end. Actually, it was not until we began to look at process that we actually reduced scrap in the more concrete setting of manufacturing. Certainly, I just have been very impressed in my life with how attention to tiny details that seem to be irrelevant to the end product end up affecting the end product very much.

Now, I want all of you to respond to Ms. Rosenthal's concern, which I consider to be absolutely real and legitimate. States are pursuing mandatory systems. My own State adopted a mandatory system. However, they have a very narrow definition of what must be reported under that mandatory system. It has to be associated with death or serious measurable disability.

So, I do not know whether the other States all have that narrow of a definition, but Ms. Rosenthal did imply that their focus primarily and that the IOM saw the mandatory system as focused primarily on that kind of an "error." Now, we all know that some of those cases that end up to be death or disability are not the result of error, they are the result of high-risk surgery and the outcome was going to be bad and this was a chance to try to change it. So, I think you have to be careful about identifying all of those reports as necessarily error-related. States are requiring all those reports so that they can look and see which are error-related, and that is useful.

Now, as I understand her testimony, and I will give her a chance to enlarge on it in a minute, but as I understand her testimony, she is saying two things. First of all, everybody needs a mandatory reporting system, we should mandate that. Second, she is saying it would create two reporting systems. Now, there is a slight contradiction in her testimony about this dual reporting system because the IOM is proposing a dual reporting system and they do overlap. There is no way of getting away from that.

So, how do you currently, in your own institutions as the system is currently developing, deal with the dual reporting? I mean, if we put this in place and this system comes up, what will be its impact on the mandatory reporting system of your State? Dr. Wood?

Dr. WOOD. Perhaps I could try to respond to that in this way.

Chairman JOHNSON. I am really expecting all of you to. I want Ms. Rosenthal to be able to enter in whenever she wants to, and she can just sort of signal that, because we need to hear this discussion about the inevitable—I mean, inevitably, this is going to be a dual reporting system. Even if you do it the way the IOM wanted, it is going to be dual. So, let us talk about that straight out and get it out and see, make sure that we do this as well as we can. Dr. Wood?

Dr. WOOD. I truly do not believe this is an either/or situation, and I agree with you, Mrs. Johnson, that having two pathways, if you will, for two different sets of problems would not be incompatible either with the IOM report or with maybe the direction that we should be heading in.

Right now, I do think mandatory reporting is a reality when we are talking about the most egregious problems. It is a reality in 13 States by State mandate, and it is also a reality for the majority of accredited hospitals in this country who are associated with the JCAHO sentinel events policy.

What we are lacking is the opportunity and the tool to bring those near-misses out so that we can get at the real opportunity for process improvement, and that is the value of a voluntary reporting relationship, in my opinion.

Chairman JOHNSON. Also for the rest of you, in those States where there is no mandatory policy, you need to talk about that, too. Mr. Segel?

Mr. SEGEL. The situation in Pennsylvania is still fluid because an act has been passed but regulations have not been issued. It will require mandatory reporting of serious incidents. By the way, a previous system existed that was mandatory but got very few reports because it was not appropriately supported and then there was deep mistrust in the system. Then the new act will define a reporting process for near-misses, as well.

I think the reason why I disagree with the statements that have been made is because the purpose of this bill is to extend some additional protection to institutions that choose voluntarily to produce information and bring it out into the open. It is not, in my view, a duplication or an undermining of what might happen in our State or any other place. It is instead creating some additional protection and safety around information that is brought out into the open, and it is voluntary, so it is voluntary to the providers, whether they choose to accept that protection in exchange for that commitment to the learning system regionally and nationally.

Chairman JOHNSON. That is an important distinction, that it is voluntary. Dr. Pardes?

Dr. PARDES. I think my colleagues have already stated it rather well. I do not see why the one necessarily has to preempt or compromise the other. The idea is to get as much information out on the table, which I think will allow us to have much more ground on which to reduce medical errors in the broader sense.

Chairman JOHNSON. Ms. Rosenthal, given the contradictory experience of JCAHO's system and MedMARx, why do you think it is a bad thing to have multiple approaches?

Ms. ROSENTHAL. I very much think there should be multiple approaches. What I was trying to clarify was that the Institute of Medicine report recommends both mandatory and voluntary systems as complementary systems that are different in scope, purpose, and function, that mandatory reporting systems are intended for the State to hold health care providers accountable for safety, for reporting specifically of those events that cause serious harm or death, whereas voluntary reporting is intended for those events that cause less harm or no harm, and there is no reason not to protect that.

I think the distinction was that if those serious events are reported into a voluntary system, then they are also going to be reported into the mandatory system, so they need to be separate——

Chairman JOHNSON. That is right. In those States that have a mandatory law, there will be two pathways. However, the majority of States do not have a mandatory law, therefore will be one pathway and at least we will begin to get them started. If we do the two-pathway process, which the IOM envisioned, perhaps we just need to make a better accommodation in this bill to assure that HHS works with each State to minimize or to make as simple as possible the collaboration of these two systems. What would be your response to that, Ms. Rosenthal?

Ms. ROSENTHAL. I think that is correct. I think the fear is that if all the attention and effort is going into voluntary reporting without support for States to do their part for mandatory reporting, then we cannot meet the IOM criteria and we cannot assure consumers that we are working to improve the health care system.

Chairman JOHNSON. How long have the State laws been in place?

Ms. ROSENTHAL. It depends. Many of them have been in place for 20 or so years, but they have been fairly dormant.

Chairman JOHNSON. See, the 20 or so years have not worked——

Ms. ROSENTHAL. Well——

Chairman JOHNSON. In Pennsylvania, or we would know more about this. So, in a sense, it is because the old mandatory systems did not work that there is such division now in the community about whether we should go mandatory or voluntary. What about the more recent bills passed by the States? What evidence do we have that they are bringing up more than just the report of the incident of death, which I think in most cases was already reported, was it not anyway? It certainly was public information.

Ms. ROSENTHAL. First of all, the reporting systems that were created many, many years ago were mostly created—intended for a different purpose, and when the Institute of Medicine called attention to this issue, they are now looking for ways to try to improve the system specifically for this purpose.

Chairman JOHNSON. So were the old systems too narrow?

Ms. ROSENTHAL. No, I think they were just focused on—they were not necessarily using the data to look for the types of things that they are looking for now.

Chairman JOHNSON. Do we understand why they did not get many mandatory reports under the old systems?

Ms. ROSENTHAL. Well, they were not developed to address medical errors, but some did report on what have come to be known as adverse events. In many cases, the requirements did not attract much attention and lay dormant until a tragic event occurred that led to media inquiries about State regulatory oversight of hospitals.

Chairman JOHNSON. What I am really asking is, what do we know about the efforts of the States to do mandatory reporting and how successful they are? My view is that we do not know a lot yet because they have not been in place very long. So, part of my reluctance is to mandate that every State do this. I would like to get a little further down the road and see how the States are doing with that. Meanwhile, I think, not to move ahead with the voluntary system which IOM also recommended would be relatively irresponsible. Do you object to moving forward with the voluntary system, or is it just that you would like us to also mandate a mandatory system on the States?

Ms. ROSENTHAL. There is no objection to voluntary, but that it be complemented with mandatory. I think that in looking at a State, often New York is the State that is used as an example of a successful system that receives more than 20,000 reports a year, which is quite a few, if you look at JCAHO receiving only 2,000 reports in 5 years from all accredited facilities nationwide.

Chairman JOHNSON. Two thousand, but it is not a lot if you look at MedMARx receiving 400,000.

Ms. ROSENTHAL. Right, but just for New York State, over 20,000 is a pretty good number. According to the States with the systems, their feeling is that this is an important opportunity for them to see what is happening within health care facilities and to monitor facilities and identify systems problems as part of their licensure process

Chairman JOHNSON. What is there in our bill that would prohibit any State that does not currently have a mandatory system from adopting a law to have a mandatory system?

Ms. ROSENTHAL. Resources, mostly, and the inclusion in this bill of information on those events that cause death and serious harm, which could have a chilling effect on the development of State mandatory reporting systems which are intended to collect this information.

Chairman JOHNSON. It is not laws. In other words, we are not putting any legal barriers up to the development of mandatory reporting at the State level, correct?

Ms. ROSENTHAL. That is correct.

Chairman JOHNSON. Yes. I understand the resource issue, but that is true in every area across the country, I mean, in every sector, and it is certainly true in this sector. Dr. Leape?

Dr. LEAPE. Madam Chairman, based on some of the excellent work of Dr. Rosenthal, I think it is a fair assessment to say that the reason State mandatory reporting systems have not worked is they have all been under-funded. Even New York, which everybody touts as being successful because they get 20,000 reports, does not have the resources to analyze those reports and make recommendations, to give feedback to do what needs to be done. Reporting without analysis and recommendations is a waste of everybody's time, and that has been the situation in State mandatory reporting systems with few exceptions.

One of the Institute of Medicine's recommendations which was acted upon was to develop a parsimonious list of reportable events, a list of events that everybody would agree are so egregious that States have a responsibility to make sure they are reported and investigated. The concept is that if the list is kept small and restricted to things that we all agree are serious, then there would be more likelihood of the State being able to insist that these be reported and to follow up and do something about them.

The fact of the matter is that very few States do much about any of these reports, and as long as that is true, hospitals are not going to report because they see no benefit from it, leaving aside all of the problems of embarrassment and legal ramifications. I think it is beyond the purview of Congress to dictate to States how much they can spend for their mandatory reporting systems.

Chairman JOHNSON. That is a problem, and one of the reasons in this bill—I mean, in my first bill, there was no setting aside in HHS of a patient safety agency department. There was also not a national databank. That is something that, in working together, in the draft before the Committee are there and they will require funding. As the Secretary pointed out, he wants to be sure he has the funding.

I think we can take responsibility for eliciting reports and for analyzing them through the process we have set forward in this bill. If we mandate on the States, we would certainly have to mandate money. We are not yet agreed as to how much this bill will cost or how we will support that effort at the Federal level. I think one really has to begin to ask, do we need 50 abilities as well as a national ability to analyze this data?

I thought your comments, I think it was Dr. Wood but I cannot quite remember now—one of you mentioned how some of the peer review organizations are providing some analysis of data from single institutions, so there is developing a conversation between those who have analytic capability on a smaller scale. That is very helpful. We do need to encourage the development of that analytical capability, and right now. I guess, as a Member of Congress, I would rather focus on the system that we need to develop for national purposes. That system has to be more encompassing on the number of incidents, the number of reports, and types of incidents and reports, because the national effort certainly has to be focused at prevention and at system change.

We will, inevitably, encompass also for those States that do not have a mandatory reporting system all of the more serious reports, as well. So, we will have to watch this over time as each system develops and work closely with the States and with offices like yours that track all the State developments. I would be happy personally to think through with you if there is any way we can foster that collaboration in this bill. Mr. Stark?

Mr. STARK. Thank you. I want to thank the panel and thank you, Ms. Rosenthal, for carrying the water for the IOM here and in the States.

I think that, just to comment on the previous questions, that in the bill before us, there probably would not be transparency for what is called sentinel events. In other words, there is no distinction in this bill between a death and a near-miss. Therefore, the deaths and disfigurements and disabling accidents would not necessarily, or might be prohibited from being transparent, and Dr. Leape, you mentioned the importance of transparency in your testimony.

The American Medical Association (AMA) Code of Medical Ethics says that significant medical complications may have resulted from the physician's mistake or judgment. In these situations, the physician is ethically required to inform the patient of all facts necessary to ensure understanding of what has concern and concern regarding legal liability which might result following truthful disclosure should not affect the physician's honesty with the patient, right? You subscribe to that, do you not? Dr. Wood does, I know. He is a big guy in the AMA.

Well, then why would it not be—what would be the objection to requiring us patients from knowing that? Would you have any objection to that, Dr. Leape? Why should it not be the law of the land that if there is a mistake, that—if I am dead, I guess I do not know who you are going to tell, but if I am seriously harmed, why should I be told?

Dr. LEAPE. I do not want to get into a metaphysical discussion about how you require people to be good, but I think that there is no question that physicians——

Mr. STARK. What little time——

Dr. LEAPE. Subscribe to the concept that the patient has a right to know everything that has happened to them, and I think we are making a lot of progress in achieving that. The idea that you can do that by legislation totally escapes me.

Mr. STARK. The idea is that if somebody did a little time for lying, for not telling the patient, it would have a meritorious effect, it seems to me, on the rest of the profession. We have got 100,000 deaths, at least, from errors related to hospitals a year. Now, nobody dies from near-misses, and we seem to be ignoring those as not being very important. I would like to work on those for a while, and it seems to me that, yes, there would very likely, although there is some literature that suggests that perhaps if hospitals and doctors deal honestly with patients up front, they might not get mad and sue later. I do not know how you know that or would not know it.

Do you not think that we should, where we have mandatory reporting, require that the patient should be informed?

Dr. LEAPE. I think what we are interested in doing is preventing injury, and the way to prevent that is to change the systems. Now, most of those 100,000 deaths were not caused by bad doctors and bad nurses. They were caused by problems in the systems. If we want people to address those, we have to make it easy for them to talk about them and we have to make it easy to address the issues. If we do not do that——

Mr. STARK. If you cannot tell the guy you hurt, who are you going to tell?

Dr. LEAPE. I think there is no question that a physician has a moral obligation to be honest with his patient, no question about it.

Mr. STARK. You do not want to make that——

Dr. LEAPE. I do not think you achieve that by legislation.

Mr. STARK. You do not want to make that a legal obligation.

Dr. LEAPE. I would not make that illegal, no.

Mr. STARK. Just so the doctors can lie, so they do not tell us?

Dr. LEAPE. Not at all. We have a lot going on to change that right now and it will change.

Mr. STARK. The patients do not—I mean, nobody gives a hoot about the patients here. It is just protecting the doctors from getting sued. That is what is the trouble with you guys.

Now, Dr. Wood, your comments on the NQF patient safety draft report, you say there should be no efforts to Federally regulate or mandate any of the safe practices on the steering committee's list until such Federal protections have been legislated and fully implemented. That is your belief, right?

Dr. WOOD. That is correct.

Mr. STARK. Okay. Now, you also indicate that this bill and its reporting protections are sufficient. So, does that mean that the HLC would support federally regulating safe practices once the reporter protections in this bill are fully implemented?

Dr. WOOD. I think I would be inclined to answer that affirmatively.

Mr. STARK. Right on. We have made some progress. Would you mind if we had in this mandatory reporting the fact that the patient ought to know when there is an accident and there ought to be, I think, a criminal penalty for not telling them, but you cannot ever know whether somebody is going to be honest with a patient. That is the trust issue we have to have.

Dr. WOOD. Mr. Stark, in getting back to your earlier questions also to Dr. Leape, I do not see anything in this bill that prohibits the health care profession from informing a patient when there has been an accident or error occurring. I think the point that I really am trying to make is that this legislation has the opportunity to actually benefit and make safer health care by, again, getting at the opportunity for process improvement.

Mr. STARK. If we could start out those near-misses that you are talking about and make those only—and I think Ms. Rosenthal would buy into this—subject to this confidentiality, leaving what I think is referred to as sentinel events, that is bad things, big bad things, leaving those under the mandatory reporting structure, the problem is in this bill there is no distinction. So, we might start to get all the bad or the sentinel stuff in and it would not be transparent and nobody would know about it and that is a danger I see. Am I seeing this right, Ms. Rosenthal? I mean, if we could somehow define that, I think the bill would be better.

Dr. WOOD. I think that a two-pronged approach like that would have a real opportunity to enhance patient safety and would be a step forward.

Mr. STARK. Thank you. Does anybody else want to add anything that will help the patients while we are here? I do think, and I want to, again, I want to thank the IOM and all the people and John Eisenberg, who years ago—I hope you will name this after him someday when we get the agency going—it is a major concern, and I know that the liability is a concern and I know that the humility of making mistakes is awful. I do not know how I know that, because politicians never make mistakes, but I do know it.

I hope that we can, and I think we have to mandate some stuff. I mean, I hope we can get the legislation. I would submit that we would not have air bags on cars if we had not passed a Federal law. I mean, I think we would still be talking about it and saying, well, it is voluntary and it costs too much. I think there are some things that are inconvenient, they are uncomfortable, they are a whole lot of things that do not fit into our making our life happy, but that are necessary.

My concerns with the bill, and I think we could perhaps straighten them out, is that we do not stop doing that, whether it is not allowing your residents to work more than 60 hours a week because they will make a mistake, or whether it is using the safe needles that we finally had to legislate to get some of the hospitals to use. Those are things that I think, sooner or later, people are not going to like. They do not like regulations. We do not like them here. Madam Chair, I think that if we can decide those major events that have to be regulated and then let the profession and the industry or the providers work on the rest until they come up, I mean, I would be happy to have them decide, but then they are going to want to do it because it may be a competitive issue. If Mayo has got to do it, then why does Johns Hopkins not have to do it? The fact is, they probably should, so go to it.

Chairman JOHNSON. I would like to come back to Dr. Woods' comment, but I had a long period to question him first. You have had a long period of questioning. I am going to turn to Congresswoman Thurman, and then if there is time, we will discuss that further, but there are a lot of questions raised by this discussion. Congresswoman Thurman?

Mrs. THURMAN. Madam Chairman and Representative Stark, I have to tell you, this has been a good discussion because this is the discussion that has been going on in this Committee between the Members, I mean, in trying to figure out how do we meet this one issue that is now on the table.

I was encouraged certainly by what Ms. Rosenthal said in the two-tier, one mandatory, in those areas, that seems to be where the States are heading and that is when there are adverse events, and then the one where we all recognize that there are some things that go on out there that potentially could cause harm, have not caused harm, but can be corrected just because we are seeing it happen over and over again.

So, I am actually very encouraged by this and I think it is what I made a comment to Secretary Thompson earlier, was that if we could get that discovered in this—maybe discovered was not the right word to use in this case, but if we could come up with that verbiage to set those two aside, I think we have probably worked out a good majority of the issue that has been on the table, quite frankly.

I guess that the only other thing I would say, and I thank Dr. Pardes for recognizing some of the work we have done on this in the money part of it. It is a huge issue for folks out there. As we all know this year, we were talking about cutting hospitals by 0.55 percent. We have now come back, thanks to HHS, with about a $10 billion appropriations on the table, but quite frankly, we are talking about a major system and the ability to talk.

Dr. Leape, I have to tell you, I did not realize it had been 40 years that this has been going on, but it really certainly tells you how we have just come to a standstill on some of these issues. It is just not acceptable. I mean, whatever we are talking about here, the bottom line is it is lives. It is about people. It is about things that can be affected in a positive way, and we are seeing that happening and we are seeing it happening because there has been some push over the last couple of years and direction to the States and others to come up with some ways to do some reporting and find out where the problems are.

If we are standing in the way of not making this where we are having a 90-percent success and only having 20-percent success, then we need to figure out how to do this. I mean, we are talking about one cost at one time to get into some compliance that would work. After that, you are on your own. Immediately, the upstart is always the hardest to get people to fall into line to do these things. Quite frankly, I think we are talking about people's lives and that, to me, is just kind of unacceptable. I would hope that after this discussion, if we look at, and I would say to the Chairwoman——

Chairman JOHNSON. If the gentlelady would yield, because there is an aspect of this discussion that I think we need to get on the table——

Mrs. THURMAN. I was just going to say, if we go to what Ms. Rosenthal has given us in the Academy, I do not know if this is a letter that you have, but it is on the second page, basically where it says the bill does not distinguish between the purpose of collecting information about medical errors that result in serious harm and those that result in minimal or no harm, that, in particular, I think, is the crux of the issue that we have been dealing with, and based on some of this conversation today, probably could take care of some of the issues we are concerned about.

Chairman JOHNSON. Ms. Rosenthal, would you prefer a system in which matters of serious errors were reported at the State level, and in a sense, non-serious errors were reported to the Federal system? Would you prefer that system?

Ms. ROSENTHAL. I am not sure I got that completely, a system where serious——

Chairman JOHNSON. In other words, would you prefer a totally bifurcated system?

Ms. ROSENTHAL. With serious events reported to mandatory State——

Chairman JOHNSON. State level.

Ms. ROSENTHAL. And near-misses, those that cause less serious harm reported to a voluntary system? Yes.

Chairman JOHNSON. Well, and the voluntary system being national and the mandatory system being State. See, to me, I think this would be a terrible error of public policy because you are going to have every State having different analytical capabilities to understand the serious incidents in their States. You are going to have no national capability to look at incidents from the different States. You are probably going to have, not necessarily, but you are going to have very varied resources for analysis and feedback from State-to-State.

It seems to me that you want a system that feeds these most serious errors up to the national level as well, and I want our—if I am going to fund this, I want to have both the little incidences and the big instances. It is from that body of knowledge that you develop system changes, and I do not object—my bill does absolutely nothing to prevent States from adopting mandatory reporting systems and moving right along the way they are. I think we need to get a little further along with that and see how useful it is and what it does. The States cannot do what we need to do, which is all of this voluntary reporting, because I want things voluntarily reported that have no risk at all but just are suppose, you know, we could do it better this way. I want people to feel that if I say, gee, we could do it better this way, that is not going to come back to haunt my institution in a court situation. Well, they should have listened to this person.

So, we have got to protect voluntary reporting if we are going to get big ideas and flexibility so you get real systems information. Now, to disconnect that, first of all, I am not sure at all that in law you could define what information we would protect and collect if you try to dissect out of that information universe the information that is associated with serious errors, and I do not know why you would want to do that.

Now, if you think we can define out that information for the voluntary system, you need to tell me what that definition would be and then justify why you think that would be a good thing, to have the Nation, the national analytical capability associated only with the less-serious data.

Ms. ROSENTHAL. Well, I think it is possible to distinguish what is classified as an adverse event or serious harm according to——

Chairman JOHNSON. Wait a minute now. See, we are not just talking about that. It is easy to say adverse event and serious harm. We are talking about the data associated with those incidents and how that data would not be under the voluntary reporting system, nor would it go to the national level.

Ms. ROSENTHAL. There has been an effort on the Federal level through the National Quality Forum to develop that list of serious events——

Chairman JOHNSON. Right.

Ms. ROSENTHAL. That would be used by States to collect that kind of information, and part of the reason that States need that data is because they are responsible for licensing health care facilities, so if they do not have that data——

Chairman JOHNSON. That is good. That is all good.

Ms. ROSENTHAL. So, if this bill makes it more difficult for States to enact those systems——

Chairman JOHNSON. It does not make it more difficult. I asked that earlier in the questioning and you said you did not see any barriers to State progress.

Ms. ROSENTHAL. Well, I think in my testimony, I tried to describe that there is some—the duplication and not distinguishing between those events that cause serious harm versus those——

Chairman JOHNSON. If you are required to report that information to the State, you report it. So, at least in all the States that have not passed a mandatory reporting requirement, which is the majority, they would be required under our law to report it to us, to report it to the—well, they would not be required, because it is voluntary, but the likelihood that they do it and the likelihood that Federal systems like JCAHO would require them is extremely great.

Ms. ROSENTHAL. It makes it more difficult for the States that do not currently have systems. If there is a system that is conflicting on the Federal level and makes it easier for those who would be reporting into a mandatory system to say, well, there is already this system, you do not need to create one on the State level, so there is——

Chairman JOHNSON. That is true, but you also acknowledge that the States have not put the resources in to analyze the data. So, if we get the data reported for the most serious things in the State and it is not analyzed and we cut that data out of the voluntary system at the national level, I mean—see, I do not have any problem with both. I am appalled that you would advocate this total bifurcation. What we want is integration, not bifurcation. We do not want side-by-side systems. We want rich reporting systems, and there is no harm in the State reporting and analyzing. Maybe some of their people will be better and that will be rich, but I see a lot of problems with bifurcation. Mr. Segel, and then——

Mrs. THURMAN. Could I——

Chairman JOHNSON. Let me let Mrs. Thurman clarify her thoughts on my thoughts, and then you can all respond to that.

Mrs. THURMAN. You can tell we have kind of been through this already once.

Chairman JOHNSON. Well, we have not been through this particular thing, and this is good.

Mrs. THURMAN. It is very important, though, I agree.

Chairman JOHNSON. Because you can have theoretical ideas, but if you cannot write them in law, you do not have a system and you do not have a law.

Mrs. THURMAN. I think part of the problem is, if you develop one at a voluntary, at the Federal level, then that takes precedence over the State. So, if the States have put this mandatory in, they send it up to the Federal and say, well, I have already done this and it is voluntary. I do not know if that is part of the problem. I mean, we supercede State law in these kinds of issues, so you could potentially undo what some of these States have already done. Is that——

Chairman JOHNSON. To that issue, though, let us get that clear, because I do not think Ms.——

Mrs. THURMAN. That is what I am asking.

Chairman JOHNSON. All right. Sorry, I thought you were saying—because I asked you this earlier, Ms. Rosenthal, so proceed. I think the question is, does this law supercede State law?

Ms. ROSENTHAL. Well, some of the—if adverse events are required to be reported—if adverse events are included in a Federal voluntary system and there is confidentiality protections for that data, if that interferes with the State mandatory system that makes that information available to the public, there could be——

Chairman JOHNSON. There is no provision in this bill that says if you report it to us, you do not have to report it to the State under the State law. There is no provision that does that. So it is true, your argument that they will have to report to two entities, that is a valid argument. To say that in any way this bill interferes with State law is really—you have to document if you are going to say that. I have said enough. Mr. Segel?

Mr. SEGEL. Maybe it would be worth putting into the legislation a specific clause that says, nothing in this bill preempts the responsibility to report under State mandatory reporting systems. Something as simple as that might solve it.

Chairman JOHNSON. Certainly, those things can be done.

Ms. ROSENTHAL. I guess what that does—I would agree with that, also, but I think what that does not address is what the IOM recommendation called for was two types of systems, with State systems funded at the national level, and I think the concern of States is that if this bill goes forward as voluntary reporting only with funding, that there will not be future funding available as recommended in the IOM report for States for the mandatory systems.

Chairman JOHNSON. With the pressure to fund prescription drugs, do you really think there is going to be very much future funding? I mean, if we can get this system funded, do you think we are going to fund State systems?

Ms. ROSENTHAL. Honestly, no.

Chairman JOHNSON. So, let us not kid ourselves. If we can get one system that clearly has to be voluntary if it is national, and it is going to be over all people, all incidents, and all providers, because most State systems are only over hospitals, most of them are not over doctors, it is my recollection, is that not true?

Ms. ROSENTHAL. The systems are for facilities, not for individual——

Chairman JOHNSON. Facilities and not for individuals. Ours is much broader than that. So, if you are going to do the big universe of reporters and the big universe of data and we can get the analytical capability to fund it, we are just not going to ever be able to do the other, and you might as well be honest about that.

So, if States have not seen that it is important to fund analysis as well as to do the political thing of requiring reporting, that is something real. Look how States are under-funding their Medicaid reimbursements. I mean, States are not doing a good job. So, if we could do a good job of this one thing, we would be ahead. Mr. Segel?

Mr. SEGEL. Congresswoman, it has been a rich discussion. I just want to say I do agree with your reading of the bill and in its importance, further, and this is really a plea to the panel, health care professionals want to report. The JCAHO reports, at the level that they are at, they are essentially out the door of hospitals but stopped because of the lack of this kind of protection extending to those reports. I think if you are able to move where the great gap has been by providing some additional protection for voluntary reporting and again, it is not protecting the underlying events or a patient's right to their record at all, but it is to be able to talk about errors and analyze and provide some additional support for that process you are going to see the floodgates open. I can guarantee it from our own experience.

The task is really to take it out of the sort of legal environment within the institutions as well as externally and allow what people are desperate to have happen internally happen, and if you conceive of it in those terms or conceive of it as taking away an excuse not to act, that is the opportunity before this panel and it is the one that health care professionals who want to do the right thing are crying out for.

Chairman JOHNSON. Dr. Wood, since you supported a dual system, you had better have a few words here.

Dr. WOOD. In responding to Congressman Stark's earlier question, I think what we really are trying to do is do anything positive that is realistically passable to improve the safety for patients. I really do believe that the more we have a mandatory requirement in the bill, the more obstacles we will have in front of us.

In my own opinion, we already have a large number—for the kind of cases that Dr. Leape was referring to earlier, the truly egregious type areas, the cases that the IOM report was trying to get to, we actually have some mechanisms in place as we exist today through JCAHO and through some State mandates, and if putting a mandatory provision in this particular bill, I can't help but feel that it will increase some of the barriers to getting it passed.

If we have the opportunity to move forward with the voluntary activity alone, to eliminate those barriers, and in order to bring those near-misses out of the woodwork, I think that would be the most positive step forward.

Chairman JOHNSON. Well, I can tell you flat out, there is no way that I can get a bill on the House Floor to pass—I am not sure I can even get it as far as the House Floor, but you cannot pass a clear unfunded mandate on the States at this time, nor would it be fair. They all have deficits. You particularly cannot do that when you have not funded anything yourself——

Dr. WOOD. Right——

Chairman JOHNSON. That covers all that vast amount of opportunity to reduce errors that they cannot reach. So, if we have to go to mandatory, then this bill is dead, no question about that. Thank you very much. I really feel like we have to——

Mrs. THURMAN. Can I just——

Chairman JOHNSON. Yes. Congresswoman Thurman?

Mrs. THURMAN. This is where some of our concern comes from. In the bill on page seven under the last, starting online 33, it talks about no limitation of other privileges. "Nothing in this section shall be construed to limit other privileges that are available under Federal or State laws that provide greater peer review or confidentiality protections than the peer review and confidentiality protections provided in this section." I think that is where some of these questions are coming from as far as the supremacy of the States and those that, in fact, would have and are addressing mandatory. That is the problem. For us who live in States and have sunshine laws and things like that, it is very difficult to go against your State legislature that have put these protections in, and particularly when you look at the kinds of pieces of legislation that are being filed every day.

I agree with Chairman Johnson in the fact that I would love to have this done so that we could get some of this information and make it national, but I also recognize that there are States out there that will continue to do this, and for us to get in their way when they have the licensing, they are going to get the phone calls in their offices, it makes it very difficult.

Chairman JOHNSON. We will certainly look at trying to clarify that nothing we are intending to do here will in any way limit the responsibility of facilities to comply with State laws. We will certainly do that.

Mrs. THURMAN. Thanks.

Chairman JOHNSON. Thank you very much for your patience and for helping us on this discussion. It is an important one. The hearing is adjourned.

[Whereupon, at 2:34 p.m., the hearing was adjourned.]

[Submissions for the record follow:]

Statement of the American Academy of Family Physicians

Introduction

This statement is submitted to the Ways and Means Health Subcommittee regarding the Chairman's mark of H.R. 4889, the Patient Safety Improvement Act of 2002. This statement is offered on behalf of the 93,500 members of the American Academy of Family Physicians (AAFP).

Support for Confidentiality Provisions in H.R. 4889 as Introduced

More than 12 times as many people are seen in primary care physicians' offices as in hospitals. Because the majority of patient encounters occur in the physicians' office, the Academy believes that the creation of a learning culture in ambulatory care settings has the capacity to improve care for the greatest number of patients. Developing such a culture depends on federal protections of confidentiality and voluntary reporting contained within the Patient Safety Improvement Act, as it was introduced.

According to the bill, reporting non-identified patient safety information to patient safety organizations would be voluntary for every level of the health care delivery system—physician, health care provider, hospital or health care system. The Academy supports the creation of patient safety reporting systems based on the voluntary reporting of non-identified data. We believe that these provisions are prerequisites to building a non-punitive quality improvement culture that focuses on preventing and correcting system failures and *not* on assigning individual or organization culpability. As the IOM study noted, "improving patient safety requires fixing the system, not fixing blame."

The bill classifies information documented, collected, or prepared for submission to a patient safety reporting system, as privileged and confidential. Furthermore, federal protections against disclosure in civil, criminal, or administrative proceedings are created unless a judge finds the release of the information meets a strong three-pronged test: that it is material to the case; that it is in the public interest; and that it is not available from any other source. The Academy appreciates the bill's treatment of sensitive information.

Concerns with H.R. 4889 and the Chairman's Mark

The Academy has concerns that the Chairman's mark contains a weakening of the federal confidentiality protections against having patient safety reports introduced into a legal proceeding. As introduced, H.R. 4889 extends federal protections against disclosure in civil, criminal, or administrative proceedings unless a judge finds the release of the information meets a strong three-pronged test: that it is material to the case; that it is in the public interest; and that it is not available from any other source. The Academy believes that these protections are essential to an effective quality improvement system. However, the current Chairman's mark would remove these protections from criminal matters. Abandoning this protection seriously jeopardizes the likelihood that health care professionals will disclose to a PSO the non-criminal errors that they see in the course of delivering medical care since reports could be subpoenaed based on the claim that they were related to a crime.

Likewise, the Academy is concerned H.R. 4889 amends the Social Security Act and places these protections under Medicare, instead of under the Agency for Healthcare Research and Quality (AHRQ) by amending the Public Health Service Act. AHRQ is the only agency dedicated to research that focuses on access to high quality, cost-effective services; and improved health status throughout the health care *system*. The Academy believes that existing error reporting systems, which are the first candidates for Patient Safety Organization (PSO) status, have existing research connections to AHRQ and see this national center for primary care research as the most appropriate place to house patient safety efforts.

The protections offered under The Patient Safety Improvement Act are available solely to physicians with Medicare billing numbers. Therefore, under the bill, primary care physicians without Medicare billing numbers need to go through the Medicare physician billing application process solely for the purpose of obtaining a billing number in order to claim federal protections for reported data. This provision alone is likely to have a chilling effect on reported data. Likewise, the Academy has concerns that the application of all Medicare fraud and abuse laws to PSOs would have a chilling effect on reporting for both physicians and the PSO itself.

Conclusion

The Academy appreciates this opportunity to submit a statement to the subcommittee and looks forward to working with you to develop effective patient safety legislation. This is a matter of continued interest to the Academy and we thank the Ways and Means Health Subcommittee for its interest in the topic.

Statement of the American College of Obstetricians and Gynecologists

The American College of Obstetricians and Gynecologists (ACOG), an organization representing nearly 45,000 physicians, commends you for your leadership to improve patient safety. As partners in women's health care, we strongly support legislation that works to eliminate health care errors and ensure quality care for every woman.

The College encourages physicians and other health care professionals to participate in a voluntary, non-punitive system to report and evaluate errors and share their experiences with others. We support the principles that provided the foundation for the Institute of Medicine's 1999 report entitled, *To Err is Human*. It is imperative that we work together to transform the health care system into a culture of safety, which focuses on information sharing to prevent adverse outcomes. We believe that information must be subject to comprehensive analysis to identify actions that will minimize the risk that reported events would recur. Likewise, we find it equally important to protect the confidentiality of both physicians and patients and to defend all information submitted to patient safety reporting systems as privileged.

One of the College's most successful programs to date is the Voluntary Review of Quality Care (VRQC) program, established in 1986. The mission of the VRQC program is to provide peer review consultations to departments of obstetrics and gynecology, assess the quality of care provided, and suggest possible alternative actions for improvement. At the request of hospitals, this program makes available two or more board-certified, practicing obstetrician-gynecologists to evaluate the hospital's clinical performance in obstetrics and gynecology. The program offers comprehensive, department-wide reviews that focus on all practitioners with obstetric-gynecologic privileges and focused reviews of an individual physician's quality of care.

During the site visit, the reviewers use various quality improvement techniques, including an evaluation based on the College's policies and publications. Based on findings revealed from hospital data, medical record review, and interviews of key hospital staff, the review team provides a confidential comprehensive final report for the hospital containing specific recommendations. These reports are valuable tools in promoting constructive changes and helping to identify potential areas for improvement of quality of care provided. Typically, the report contains recommendations on how to improve the system, adopt new programs, and address the hospital's particular concerns.

Programs like the VRQC serve as the foundation to our efforts to ensure quality care. This successful program, however, is only one of the many tools we offer our physicians. For three decades, the College has published a line of publications to inform and assist our physicians who participate in peer review and quality improvement activities. Our 2000 volume, *Quality Improvement in Women's Health Care*, is intended to serve as a primer for obstetricians and gynecologists starting or managing quality improvement programs within their respective hospitals. Because we believe that our role as a medical specialty society is to serve as a catalyst for improvement, we continue to reach out to our physicians through postgraduate continuing medical education courses as well.

Thank you, Madam Chairwoman, for your leadership on this important issue and for the Subcommittee's attention to patient safety. ACOG appreciates the opportunity to present our concerns for the panel's consideration. The College looks forward to working with you as we push for a meaningful solution to ensure greater patient safety in the delivery of quality health care for every woman.

Statement of the American College of Physicians-American Society of Internal Medicine

The American College of Physicians-American Society of Internal Medicine (ACP–ASIM), representing more than 115,000 internal medicine physicians and medical students, is the nation's second largest medical association. The ACP–ASIM commends Chairwoman Nancy L. Johnson for her leadership on the issue of patient safety and for holding this hearing as well as the hearing on March 7.

The findings of the late 1999 Institute of Medicine (IOM) report "To Err is Human: Building a Safer Health System" are as dramatic and unacceptable now as they were two and a half years ago. The number of injuries and deaths from medical errors is open to some dispute, but there is universal agreement that the number is unacceptably high. Since the report was issued, both government and the private sector have made significant efforts to improve safety in the healthcare system, but much remains to be done.

The College accepted the IOM's challenge to the medical profession by undertaking an ambitious effort to provide our members and other physicians with the information and tools they need to create a safer healthcare system.

The ACP–ASIM quickly identified the need to address patient safety in the outpatient setting. Care is increasingly being delivered in ambulatory settings while most of the research has focused on errors in the hospital. The College embarked on a multi-year, multifaceted initiative, "The Other Side of the Quality Equation," to raise physician awareness of quality issues and facilitate physician behavior that is likely to diminish the occurrence of medical errors. The cornerstone of this Agency for Healthcare Research and Quality (AHRQ)-supported program is the development of a patient safety curriculum to teach physicians how to achieve patient safety in the ambulatory setting.

In addition to the courses being given at state chapter scientific meetings, a web-based interactive learning tool, PSILC (the Patient Safety Interactive Learning Community), has been developed for physicians to review courses and participate in discussions online. The effectiveness of these interventions will be measured through surveys addressing awareness, attitudes and reported change in safety behavior.

Beyond the College's efforts to provide physicians with significant patient safety education opportunities, the ACP–ASIM has strongly advocated for confidentiality protections to encourage voluntary reporting. We also support a strong national leadership role for the Center for Patient Safety in the development of uniform reporting methods and analysis of patient safety data.

Confidentiality Protections for Voluntary Reporting

The IOM report found that medical errors are the result of problems in the healthcare system, not of individuals. It states "The focus must shift from blaming individuals for past errors to a focus on preventing future errors by designing safety in the system." Medical errors often are complex events resulting from a series of undetected mishaps. To identify, correct and prevent medical errors, collaboration among health care professionals, administrators, and institutions is required. This cannot be done in a system where the fear of litigation is pervasive. Neither can it be done in a medical culture that discourages discussion of mistakes and the inevitable human error is a source of shame.

The College supports the expansion of peer-review and confidentiality protections to encourage providers and others in the healthcare system to come forward with vital information needed to make improvements. Information that is developed with respect to system shortcomings (root-cause analysis) and subsequent analysis to prevent such errors in the future should not be "discoverable information" used in litigation. However, this privilege should not interfere with disclosure of information that is otherwise available.

The chairman's mark limits protections to civil and administrative proceedings and appropriately excludes criminal proceedings. In addition, disclosures are permissible in a disciplinary proceeding if the disclosure is material to the proceeding, within the public interest and not available from any other source. Since the rules that govern disciplinary hearings vary substantially, it would be useful to address whether this limitation creates a loophole sufficiently large to discourage reporting of medical errors. The challenge is to strike a balance between the need for confidentiality to encourage reporting and the public's right to information that will provide protection from incompetent providers.

A Strong Role for AHRQ in Patient Safety

The legislation establishes a strong role for AHRQ's Center for Patient Safety. The Agency will continue to take the federal lead on research, evaluation and demonstrations on patient safety either directly or through grants. The Center will certify patient safety organizations, defined in the bill as private or public organizations that collect and analyze voluntary reports and develop and disseminate information on best practices in patient safety. The Center will establish a National Patient Safety Database to collect and analyze non-identifiable data. The Agency has built an impressive record in patient safety and this legislation allows that legacy to continue.

Medical Information Technology Board (MITB)

The bill establishes a new Medical Information Technology Board (MITB) to report on best practices in medical information technology and methods for implementing interoperability (e.g., compatibility of information technology architecture) standardization and records security. The Board is required to report to the Secretary after 30 months and to report each year for two years on advances in information technology, best practices and on private sector efforts to implement interoperability standards.

Advances in medical technology will play an enormous role in improving clinical care and efficiencies in the healthcare system. ACP–ASIM recommends that the Board meet on an ongoing basis beyond the 30 months specified in order to keep pace with the rapidly evolving field of informatics and be evaluated for permanent status after a three-year period.

The bill establishes a diverse board of 17 members, including staff representatives from the Centers for Medicare and Medicaid Services, AHRQ, IOM and public health agencies, and representatives with expertise in informatics from industry and educational institutions. Significantly, the bill also includes "individual and institutional health care clinical providers." We strongly support the inclusion of clinicians who can provide a practical assessment of what is feasible in day-to-day practice. We also suggest that the Board draw upon the expertise of existing organizations such as the American Medical Informatics Association and Health Level Seven (HL7), an American National Standards Institute-accredited Standards Developing Organization. It would be a significant contribution if the Board could facilitate communication and coordination among myriad organizations in the field of informatics.

Finally, the number one goal among the six enumerated for the Board is to maximize positive outcomes in clinical care, including decision support for diagnosis and care. The College has invested significantly in a decision support tool, the "Physicians' Information and EducationResource (PIER)," and continues to expand the electronic Web-based resource. Modules are available now on the diagnosis and treatment of diseases such as lymphoma and asthma. Strides in healthcare quality will be realized through medical informatics tools that provide physicians with evidence-based guidance at the point of care.

Conclusion

It would be a significant accomplishment for the Committee to report legislation that could be passed in this Congress. Confidentiality protections for patient safety data and a strong role for AHRQ would result in improved safety and quality in the healthcare system.

Statement of the American Medical Association

On behalf of our physician and medical student members, the American Medical Association (AMA) applauds Chairwoman Johnson's continuing leadership to improve patient safety and quality of health care in our nation through federal legislation that would remove the barriers that prevent the reporting and analysis of health care errors. The AMA shares Chairwoman Johnson's goal, and supports the Chairwoman's bill, H.R. 4889 (the "Patient Safety Improvement Act of 2002"), as introduced on June 6, 2002. We do, however, have concerns about the draft chairman's mark of the legislation which are discussed below. We submit this statement as a supplement to our March 7, 2002, Statement for the Record to the Ways and Means Health Subcommittee, which provides a detailed account of the myriad efforts on behalf of the AMA and other public and private health care organizations to improve patient safety and health care quality.

We believe that H.R. 4889, as introduced, would provide a framework by which our nation's health care system could more effectively advance patient safety initiatives and further promote the reporting and analysis of health care errors. Such a framework was envisioned by the Institute of Medicine (IOM) in its 1999 report, *To Err is Human: Building a Safer Health System.* In that report the IOM recommended that "Congress should pass legislation to extend peer review protections to data related to patient safety and quality improvement that are collected and analyzed by health care organizations for internal use or shared with others solely for purposes of improving safety and quality." The IOM also noted that a federal approach is required because "many current state peer review statutes ... may not protect data about errors shared in collaborative networks, especially across state lines, or reported to voluntary reporting systems."

Concerns About the Draft Chairman's Mark of H.R. 4889

Upon reviewing a draft of the chairman's mark of H.R. 4889 (dated August 2, 2002), we noted several changes to the original language. One of these changes that raises concerns would alter the scope of the confidentiality and legal protections for the unique "patient safety data" that would be reported to a "patient safety organization." Section 1182 in H.R. 4889, as introduced, extends the federal confidentiality and legal protections to a "civil, criminal, or administrative" subpoena and proceeding. The draft chairman's mark would limit the protections to a "civil or administrative" subpoena and proceeding.

The reporting of a criminal act is a fundamental requirement under state and federal laws and should not in any way be limited. The AMA believes that discovering adverse patient safety events that occur as a result of a criminal act is an inherent benefit of a patient safety system. The original language in H.R. 4889 (in section 1182) would allow any information about criminal behavior that is uncovered or otherwise discovered by a "patient safety organization" to be disclosed to the appropriate "health care provider" (hospital, clinic, etc.), which must then report such crimes under numerous existing state and federal laws.

For criminal or disciplinary proceedings, the original language of H.R. 4889 (in section 1182) already allows for the disclosure of "patient safety data" in situations where such data would be "(A) material to the proceeding; (B) within the public interest; and (C) not available from any other source." **Therefore, the protections in the original legislation would in no way limit or affect the availability of any information or evidence that is currently available under existing law. More important, maintaining the legal protections in the original language could result in criminal behavior being identified by "patient safety organizations" sooner or where it might have altogether been missed.**

The AMA is concerned about the provision in section 1182(h), which would treat patient safety organizations as business associates under the Department of Health and Human Services Privacy Rule promulgated pursuant to the Health Insurance Portability and Accountability Act of 1996 (HIPAA). The provision would also deem activities of "patient safety organizations" to be health care operations of health care providers under the Privacy Rule. This could be problematic for physicians and other health care providers.

HIPAA only applies to "covered entities" (all health care providers, including physicians and hospitals, health plans and clearinghouses). The Privacy Rule requires "covered entities" to ensure that any patient information disclosed to business associates (accountants, consultants, billing companies, etc., and other entities that may not be covered by HIPAA) remains protected. Covered entities must enter into or amend written contracts with their business associates, correct or report any known wrongful use or disclosure of patient information made by a business associate, and ultimately mitigate any harm caused by such use or disclosure. These business associate provisions clearly attempt to stretch the regulatory reach of the rule by placing on physicians extra burdens and liabilities with respect to the privacy practices of those who fall outside the rule's reach.

The only purpose of the business associate provisions is to extend privacy protections to patient information passed on to entities not covered by the Privacy Rule. Yet, the chairman's mark would already require "patient safety organizations" to maintain the confidentiality of any patient information that is disclosed to them by "health care providers" in the process of reporting. Therefore, it seems unnecessary to also require "health care providers" to first negotiate a written contract with a "patient safety organization" before any information is disclosed, not to mention placing extra responsibility and liability on "health care providers" for a potential privacy breach by a "patient safety organization." This could serve as a strong disincentive to participate in a reporting system.

We recognize that "health care providers" must obtain a patient authorization under the Privacy Rule prior to any disclosures of patient information that fall outside of treatment, payment or health care operations, *unless otherwise permitted* by the Privacy Rule. Although treating "patient safety organizations" as business associates and deeming their activities "health care operations" eliminates the need for prior authorization, it triggers the need for business associate agreements. We believe it would be much less burdensome for "health care providers" if the chairman's mark could instead provide that reporting errors to a "patient safety organization" by "health care providers" would be a permitted disclosure under the Privacy Rule.

This could be accomplished by providing that: "For purposes of applying the regulations promulgated pursuant to 264(c) of the Health Insurance Portability and Accountability Act of 1996 (Public Law 104–191; 110 Stat. 2033), a disclosure of patient safety data under this section made by a provider to a patient safety organization shall be treated as a permissible disclosure for public health activities for which an authorization or opportunity to agree or object is not required." The result would be that voluntary reporting of "patient safety data" would be a permitted disclosure under section 164.512 of the Privacy Rule. That section provides exceptions to the general requirement to obtain prior authorization for a disclosure of patient information for various public health and safety purposes, including voluntary reporting of adverse events related to FDA-regulated products.

The AMA is pleased that section 1183 of the chairman's mark would place the "Center for Patient Safety" under the Director of the Agency for Healthcare Research and Quality (AHRQ). This change places such Center in the appropriate government agency to conduct patient safety research and quality improvement. Congress recognizes the AHRQ's leadership role in improving patient safety. In December 1999, the Healthcare Research and Quality Act of 1999 (P.L. 106–129) was enacted into law to reauthorize the AHRQ (formerly the Agency for Health Care Policy and Research). In Section 912(c) of this law, Congress directed AHRQ to conduct and support research and build private-public partnerships to: "(1) identify the causes of preventable health care errors and patient injury in health care delivery; (2) develop, demonstrate, and evaluate strategies for reducing errors and improving patient safety; and (3) disseminate such effective strategies throughout the health care industry." We recommend that the AHRQ be consulted regarding this language, as well as the activities currently underway within the AHRQ's Center for Quality Improvement and Patient Safety (CQuIPS).

The AMA is committed to continuing and redoubling our efforts to work with Congress and our partners in the health care system to achieve a system in which patients are assured of safe, quality health care. The AMA appreciates the opportunity to provide our comments on the chairman's mark to H.R. 4889 and commend Chairwoman Johnson and this committee for focusing on needed improvements in patient safety and quality of care.

AMERICAN MEDICAL GROUP ASSOCIATION
ALEXANDRIA, VIRGINIA 22314
September 9, 2002

The Honorable Nancy J. Johnson
Chairwoman, Health Subcommittee
House Committee on Ways and Means
1136 Longworth HOB
Washington, DC 20515–6438

Dear Congresswoman Johnson:

On behalf of the American Medical Group Association (AMGA), I am pleased to write in support of your bill, H.R. 4889, "The Patient Safety Improvement Act of 2002." We appreciate your commitment to this critical issue and for holding this hearing.

As you are aware, AMGA is an association that represents some of the nation's largest and most prestigious, physician-directed medical groups organized as integrated health care delivery systems. The members of AMGA deliver health care to more than 50 million patients in 40 states, including 15 million capitated lives. The average AMGA member group has 186 physicians and 12 satellite locations. Member groups include the Mayo Foundation, the Cleveland Clinic, the Palo Alto Medical Foundation, the Henry Ford Health System, the Ochsner Clinic, the Lahey Clinic and, in your own state, the Connecticut Surgical Group. AMGA's mission is to shape the health care environment by advancing high quality, cost-effective, medically safe, patient-centered and physician-directed health care.

AMGA supports the sound provisions contained in your bill. We would request, however, that you further strengthen the intent of "Health Care Provider" under Definitions (Part D Section b.3). Specifically, the definition of "Health Care Provider," as currently set forth in your bill under subsections (A) and (B), appears to be related only to those practitioners who are associated with hospitals, skilled nursing facilities, home health agencies, etc. For the sake of clarity and inclusiveness, we would request that you add a subsection that reads:

"C" a physician (as defined in section 1861(r) of the Social Security Act;

"D" any other person who is engaged in the delivery of medical or other health care services (as defined in section 1861(s) (1) and (2) of such Act) in a State and who is required by the State law or regulation to be licensed or certified by the State to engage in the delivery of such services in the State;

"E" any other person or entity specified in regulations by the Secretary after public notice and comment.

As you know, the settings in which physicians practice have become quite varied and, therefore, it is important to acknowledge the demographic diversity of today's medical practitioners as an integral part of your legislation.

AMGA also applauds your clarification of key issues regarding the confidential and voluntary nature of the reporting and collection of patient safety data. AMGA strongly advocates a ". . . national, voluntary, confidential and protected reporting system that is non-regulatory." Additionally, AMGA advocates that "public reporting of such events should focus on the implementation of effective safety practices and the means by which they may be maintained by the provider and the patient."

In previous forums, AMGA has conveyed the need for all health organizations to instill a "culture of safety" in order to improve upon the assurance of safety of care for patients. Your new bill accomplishes this concept in a legislative mode that is instructive, objective and responsible.

Thank you for your continued dedication to the access, quality and reasonable cost of health care for our patients as well as the concomitant re-institution of professional respect and fairness for our practitioners. Please do not hesitate to let us know if we may be of further assistance. We look forward to working with you and your staff to move this bill forward.

Sincerely yours,

DONALD W. FISHER, PH.D.
President and Chief Executive Officer

Attachments
AMGA Statement on Patient Safety
Information on AMGA's Initiative, "Safety Collaborative for the Outpatient Environment" (SCOPE)
Cc: Members of Health Subcommittee

American Medical Group Association

Statement on Patient Safety

Members of the American Medical Group Association (AMGA) are committed to providing the highest quality of healthcare, using advanced and proven technologies in a safe and effective manner. An emphasis on patient safety is a primary aspect of quality management processes within organized systems of care. Systems, here, are the imperfect consequence of human design and maintenance. We believe continuous efforts to improve processes of care in order to eliminate medical errors are both an absolute necessity and the responsibility of all healthcare providers. AMGA supports policies that promote a comprehensive strategy to improve patient safety by creating environments encouraging organizations to identify errors, preserve confidentiality, evaluate causes and take appropriate actions to improve on future performance.

Furthermore, AMGA believes that methodical approaches to the prevention of injuries due to medical care hold the first promise for the prevention of adverse events. Strategies to prevent errors must become an integral part of the broad continuum of care improvement. This continuum presently includes methodical processes, outcomes management, patient satisfaction measurements, improved clinical techniques and innovations, peer review, information sharing among clinicians and patients and a commitment to details. Patient safety is best promoted within organizations that are vigilant and sensitive to the gravity of even the smallest error indicative of a potentially harmful process.

Patient-oriented organizations continually improve their capacities by using error sensitive management as a model for improvement. Such organizations surface errors when they occur, implement recovery strategies to mitigate harm and develop strategies to prevent repeat occurrences. Learning derived from such organizational introspection promotes continuous improvements of delivered products.

To improve patient safety, all health care organizations must instill a "culture of safety" that focuses the organization's care processes and workforce on improving the assurance of safety of care for patients. Safety must be an explicit organizational goal that is demonstrated by the strong direction and involvement of the governance, management and clinical leadership of the organization. Meaningful patient safety programs must include defined program objectives, personnel, adequate budgets and regular oversight and assessment by governance.

The standardization of treatment processes targeted to the highest quality outcomes and the avoidance of mistakes has been an integral part of AMGA's group practice model of care. Examples of how AMGA members have been active in managing patient safety include:

1. Reducing medical errors through process improvement and enhancing patient services as the major focus areas of quality improvement areas;

2. Minimizing medication errors, especially common for elderly patients taking 12–20 different daily medications, by instituting protocols for new hospital admissions and protocols for patient medication management when the patient is transferred to another facility or discharged to home;

3. Monitoring and investigating "sentinel" events (adverse medical occurrences which are unexpected, but potentially preventable as occurrences) as an active part of the group's norm in practice routines.

AMGA believes that health care providers have a professional and ethical obligation to inform patients and their families about events that lead to adverse events and injuries. Furthermore, we believe that improvements in patient safety can best be achieved through a national, voluntary, confidential and protected reporting system that is non-regulatory. Public reporting of such events should focus on the implementation of effective safety practices and the means by which they may be maintained by the provider and the patient. Lastly, legislative measures emphasizing patient safety should include provisions to reform the current culture of unbridled malpractice litigation.

In summary, AMGA advocates that:

1. Health care organizations and their professional providers should make continuous improvements of patient safety an overt and explicit objective—This can done by establishing patient safety programs, including medication safety practices, beginning at the most senior levels of responsibility and including defined executive leadership, responsibility and oversight.

2. Patient safety programs should:

- provide strong, clear and visible attention to safety issues;
- implement voluntary, non-punitive systems for reporting errors and analyzing errors within their organizations;
- incorporate well-understood safety principles such as, standardizing and simplifying equipment, supplies, and processes; and,
- establish interdisciplinary team training programs for providers that incorporate proven methods of team training, such as simulation.

3. Voluntary, non-punitive protocols for reporting adverse events can most readily be implemented throughout entire organizations by incorporation of incentives structured to promote error detection and notification while minimizing punitive fears.

Last updated: February 8, 2001

Statement of the American Nurses Association

The American Nurses Association (ANA) appreciates the opportunity to share our concerns about patient safety and medical errors. This issue is one of great importance to the nursing profession. As front line health care workers, nurses have substantial contributions to make in the effort to reduce health care error. ANA is the only full-service professional organization representing the nation's 2.7 million registered nurses (RN), including staff nurses, nurse practitioners, clinical nurse specialists, certified nurse midwives and certified registered nurse anesthetists through its 54 constituent member nurses associations. ANA submits this statement as a supplement to our March 7, 2002 testimony to the House Ways and Means Health Subcommittee. On that statement, ANA made several recommendations towards reducing medical errors.

First ANA believes it must address a crisis issue affecting all of us in the health care community. The nursing shortage has reached epidemic proportions. A recent survey by the American Hospital Association reports that hospitals are currently attempting to fill at least 126,000 vacant RN positions. The demand for nurses will increase by 25.6 percent between 2000 and 2010, this is more than 10 percent greater than the average growth across all professions. Adequate registered nurses in the hospitals and at the bedside make a difference in patient outcomes. Studies show that where there are more nurses, there are lower mortality rates, shorter lengths of stay, better care plans, lower costs and fewer medical errors.

The majority of medical errors do not result from individual recklessness, but from basic flaws in the way the health delivery system is organized. Stocking patient-care units in hospitals, for example, with certain full-strength drugs—even though they are toxic unless diluted—has resulted in deadly mistakes. Illegible writing in medical records has resulted in administration of a drug for which the patient has a known allergy. Our evolving and increasingly complex health care system often lacks adequate coordination and appropriate systems to ensure patient safety.

Despite increasing evidence that systems fail, institutions are continuing to assign and emphasize individual "blame" for errors, misjudgements and patient dissatisfaction. Hospital systems and administrators are assuming that the appropriate way to deal with the complexity of errors made in the delivery of health care is to manage the workers—through oversight and discipline—as opposed to identifying and resolving the true problem in the spirit of partnership. ANA has long advocated for investigation of system changes that may result in egregious errors by individual practitioners, noting that health care systems have downsized, restructured and reorganized to the point where processes, initially put in place to protect the public, are breaking down.

As these systems increasingly are failing to protect patients, the severity of discipline applied to individual providers for mistakes is increasing. Health care organizations must approach problem solving strategies through shared accountability and partnership for quality improvement. A shared accountability approach diminishes focus on individual blaming and enhances long-range process improvements.

ANA supports the concept of a Patient Safety Organization (PSO). Such an organization would provide a focal point for safety and quality activities by focusing on safety issues applicable to the full range of providers and health delivery systems. This entity must include adequate representation by nurses and other health professionals who are the front-line individuals in patient care.

This PSO must support research to determine what factors lead to errors. Specifically, the PSO must be charged with collecting data on organizational practices and other factors that may be associated with the occurrence of errors. In our current knowledge, no one can state with any certainty what practices could or are more likely to lead to errors. Some practices are more obvious than others. For example, bad handwriting or open stock of certain powerful drugs have been observed to be the cause for errors in health care delivery. Other casual factors that may contribute to health care errors may not be as apparent. For example, relationship between system errors and appropriate nurse staffing.

Inadequate or inappropriate staffing may mean too few registered nurses, lack of appropriate training or orientation for an RN assigned to the unit or inappropriate use of unlicensed personnel. Adequate numbers of staff are necessary to reach a safe level of patient care services. Ongoing evaluation and bench marking related to staffing are necessary elements in the provision of quality care. At a minimum, the PSO should collect data related to: average ratio of patients to registered nurses and licensed practical nurses, and unlicensed personnel, measures which differentiate between severity of patient illness, mortality and morbidity rates, readmission rates, incidence of post-discharge professional care, and length of stay, in order to examine the relationship of these variables to occurrence of health care errors.

Another issue that the PSO should examine is the relationship between the error rates and continuous hours worked by health care professionals. Just as there is concern about the number of hours worked by medical residents, ANA has become increasingly concerned by hospitals increased reliance on the use of overtime, particularly mandatory overtime, by its registered nurse staff. In today's health care workplace, 16 hour shifts are becoming increasingly commonplace and 24 hour shifts are not unheard of. Too many hospitals have come to rely on the use of overtime as a substitute for adequate supply of staff.

In reference to the issue of voluntary reporting the ANA supports the call for a nationwide mandatory reporting system under which health care systems would be responsible for reporting medical errors to state governments. Currently, about a third of all states have such a system in place. ANA would argue however that such a system of reporting and tracking adverse events must not only maintain data on when the errors are occurring, but include information on what organizational variables are responsible for the errors.

In addition, ANA maintains that nurses must be able to speak out about quality-of-care problems without fear of retaliation or the loss of their jobs. Patient advocacy is at the heart of nurses' professional commitment. In turn, patients depend on nurses to ensure that they receive proper care. Patients must be assured that nurses and other health care professionals, acting within the scope of their expertise, will be able to speak for them without fear of reprisal.

Current whistle-blowing laws remain a patchwork of incomplete coverage. This lack of coverage leaves many nurses fearing reprisals such as dismissal, harassment and blacklisting. This lack of a blame-free reporting system prevents many nurses from taking the risk of trying to protect their patients' health and safety. In order to allow nurses to function as successful patient advocates, effective whistle blower protection for nurses who report unsafe patient care must be enacted.

ANA strongly supports any effort that makes patient safety a coordinated focused element of the health care system. The establishment of safety programs must include balanced and appropriate representation of the key players and this means more than token nursing representation. Nurses are pivotal to improving patient outcomes and excellent evaluators of the work environment for deficits and solutions for quality improvements. There must be clear responsibility at the top levels of associations and organizations to make sure that needed practices are articulated and implemented.

Madam Chairman, the membership of the ANA wishes to thank you again for this opportunity to comment on this important issue. We look forward to working with you on legislation that creates an environment that supports both the patients and health care providers and assures safe quality patient care.

BIOMEDICAL METATECHNOLOGY INC.
AMHERST, NEW YORK 14226
September 8, 2002

To: Congresswoman Nancy L. Johnson (R–CT)
Chairman, Subcommittee on Health of the Committee on Ways and Means

Re: Testimony for hearing on legislation to reduce medical errors

To: Congresswoman Nancy L. Johnson (R–CT)
Chairman, Subcommittee on Health of the Committee on Ways and Means

If the subcommittee is determined to drastically cut the error rate in medical services, it should know this fact:

It is now technically feasible—and highly cost-effective—to cut the error rates by 50% or more.

In my view the only real question is whether it is politically feasible to do so.

I always speak as an individual, not for an organization. My name is Irwin D. Bross. I have been a biostatistician, cancer researcher and public health scientist for more than half a century. I don't include my CV because it is in Who's Who in Medicine and Healthcare.

How can we cut the error rates in medical services by 50% and thereby prevent much unnecessary suffering—and save many billions of dollars a year in medicare and health in medicaid and health insurance costs?

The basic idea is simple: Simply exploit our existing computer and off-the-shelf software resources to create statewide or nationwide medical databases which would serve the public interest rather professional or corporate interests.

One example will show what I mean. Here is my letter which was printed in the Buffalo News (9/19/2002):

> Secure database is feasible for patients
>
> In his column, "Pursuit of privacy may interfere with patient care," Dr. Mike Merrill said, "The privacy instinct ... comes partly from a Puritanical shame." In fact, the current emphasis of privacy advocates is mainly on the misconduct of doctors who permit confidential medical records to be used by various predators—including drug companies, marketing departments of corporations and other unauthorized people. The medical profession does show an interest in keeping patient records private when it comes to malpractice lawyers.
>
> Merrill is quite right when he says, "Given the informational deficiencies in the current health care system, adding new, more rigorous standards ... can only worsen care." On the other hand, correcting those informational deficiencies by providing a single, secure, state database for all patient data that is accessible only to authorized people would compensate for the privacy restrictions.
>
> A master statewide database has been technologically feasible for at least five years. It would save many lives in emergency situations, such as the side-effects

of multiple drug interactions. Robotic programs operating within the system could actually prevent many such side-effects. Uploads and downloads can be made secure.

Is it the privacy advocates who have successfully blocked such informational upgrades, or is it the doctors and the rest of the health care system?

As you can see, the basic idea really is relatively simple: Exploit our existing computer and off-the-shelf software resources to create statewide or nationwide medical databases which would serve the public interest rather professional or corporate interests. Use technical tricks like "data bots" to constantly "patrol" the databases and which look for the situations where "human errors" are likely to occur. When potential trouble is found, then trained paramedicals can look into it. For example, they can warn the primary physician when a patient is taking multiple drugs where dangerous interactions may occur.

The legislation to do the job should (1) state that its purpose is to cut the error rate by at least 50% within 5 years, (2) authorize the secure databases which would be used for this purpose, and (3) fund at least one test database for this purpose.

In New York State, this could be done mainly by consolidating existing databases in some area and I would estimate that it could be done for less than $20 million per year for a five year period.

The subcommittee should be careful (and perhaps innovative) in seeking advice on cutting error rates.

If the committee chooses to rely on lobbyists or professional groups or "do-gooder activists" for advice on computerized systems designed to cut the currently high error rates in medical services, it will get advice that is advantageous to these advisors rather to ordinary Americans with health problems.

What it needs to do is to convene a panel which would act like a grand jury: It would consist of ordinary citizens who listen to conflicting testimony from "expert" witnesses and then use common sense to make its "verdict".

In other words, any persons who may be in conflict of interest (i.e., have a special interest in the issue) would be excluded from the panel. This is the opposite of the "blue ribbon" panels ordinarily convened for medical issues. These have rarely operated in the public interest and a different approach to getting advice is worth trying.

My main point, however, is that if the committee wants to cut the error rates in medical services by 50% or more, it is now technologically feasible to do this within five years.

IRWIN D. BROSS, PH.D.
President

LOS ANGELES, CALIFORNIA 90083–0008
September 10, 2002

Mr. Joel White
C/O Committee on Ways and Means
Subcommittee on Health
1136 Longworth Office Building
Washington, DC 20515

Re: Statement and commentary

HR 4889: Patient Safety Improvement Act of 2002

Please note that the following is being written on behalf of my father, RONALD LEE BONNER (1941–2000). The title of my presentation is "Gone But Not Forgotten: The Eradication of Dirty Lab Coat Secrets".

Dear Health Subcommittee:

It is with earnest hope that by coming forward and speaking out about how this bill would impact me; that it would serve as a catalyst to enable other families to tell their stories about bad medical experiences. While my story on behalf of my father is no different than 1,000 other stories of similar note, I offer his story as just one example of what happens frequently without mention.

Everyday, countless people die unexpectedly in the midst of medical treatment/mistakes. These senseless deaths hardly register a beep or a blip on our collective EEG consciousness. Sure, surviving family members know when something doesn't feel right about what they're being told. However, more often than not they're told their medical interpretation of the results are somehow skewed. Doctors attempt to console grieving relatives in terms of a Phase I, Phase II, and Phase III analysis of their work. Yet, all the while never completely justifying their approach to methodology to the satisfaction of the listener.

Many times doctors pump themselves full of their version of a medical truth serum and employing tactics in a vain, emotionless attempt to explain their deadly actions to an unsuspecting public. Families are indiscriminately, and pointedly coaxed into silence for fear of reprisals or being mocked. Doctors try and make people feel uneducated and dumb against their verbose and often ethereal language. Over and over again this scenario is played out in sharp contrast to their starch white clean image of perfection. The backdrop to this whole drama is a scrim-dividing wall, separating self-described "mistake-free" doctors away from the inquiring minds of patients and their families. I urge the members of the Committee not to allow, "The Patients Safety Act Bill" (HR 4889), to become shrouded in as much mystery as some forms of patient healthcare. This bill must proceed in a fair and equitable manner for all involved; while not forgetting the very people it was meant to protect.

Bill 4889 should not be thought of as a lopsided pendulum never quite swinging evenly in favor of patients as well as the doctors it already serves. Nor should you be hasty in passing the bill without some changes which I will expound upon, shortly. Gone are the days when our nation's citizens will accept and be pacified by intellectually numbing, "broken limb", half-hearted excuses for doctors fateful decisions and false chart remarks. In order for this bill to become successful it must include a level of sanctioning and accountability (Proposed Change #1). One needs to include disciplinary action if you're going to speak of a bill whose underlying theme is patient safety!! The public will not stand by and idly allow our loved ones to be swept away in a morass of "Dirty Lab Coat" secrets. The only way to place "systematic steps to reduce the incidence" [1] of errors is to send a clear message to the medical community that such miscalculations will no longer be tolerated. The best way to accomplish this is through corrective action.

Contrary to what is suggested in Section 1185 of this proposed bill I think we should create (Proposed change #2) "methods which would constitute national practice guidelines".[2] Other countries have them, why not the United States? The repeated squelching of critical safety errors have led and will continue to lend itself to the subsequent suppression and washing away of gross mistakes and errors the kinds of which led to my father's death. Visualize this picture if you will:

a) A male patient being given pregnancy and breast cancer medicine.

b) A patient on 6 diuretics compacted with in a six-month period.

c) For that matter a CHF patient being prescribed foot cream. "Go Figure" on this one.

d) A patient suddenly with a need of multiple ambulance/emergency generated pick ups and (coincidently) having doctors involved in his case who (ironically) specialize in E.R. care (how convenient!!); when at no other time in my father's life has he ever been ill enough to warrant such health scares.

e) Psychiatric meds given to him when he openly questioned the treatment he was receiving, and no doctor of appropriate degreed capacity (specifically a psychiatric doctor) on his team. This in turn generated comments of him being in an "altered state of consciousness" to justify what was wrongfully written and assessed in his medical records.

f) One medication in particular XELODA, had warnings against its continued use for at least 6 months prior (to prescription to my father) informing doctors of the mandate for immediate discontinuance.

g) The possibility the doctors knew in advance that certain drugs would produce numerous readmissions thus boosting their medical intervention at almost the same alarming rate as his continual hospitalizations.

h) The combination of poly-pharmacy left my father without enough blood circulating through his body to even maintain adequate oxygen flow.

In an earlier speech our current president asked us "all to pray for this great nation of ours".[3] His own father once said, "Read my lips" [4]; to which my late grandmother, Sadie Mike countered with, "Hear what I say!" [5]. To merge some of those same words and ideas I pray upon the members of this Committee to heed my words. Make no mistake. I meant every bit of what has been presented here before you, today. Your bill is palatable overall but some changes are in order.

---

[1] Quote taken from H.R. Bill 4889.
[2] Quote taken from Section 1185 of H.R. Bill 4889.
[3] (Current) President Bush, in an earlier speech.
[4] (Former/Elder) President Bush, famous quote from the 1980's.
[5] Popular saying of the late Mrs. Sadie Ann Mike.

Thank you one and all for allowing me to present these remarks to you on this most important of bills.

Very truly yours,

DENA J. BONNER

CENTENNIAL, COLORADO 80016
September 5, 2002

Sirs:

I have recently retired after 30 years of medical practice in the specialty of Otolaryngology/Head and Neck Surgery. I served in a variety of roles during this time: Surgery Chief, Quality Assurance Committee, Chief of Medical Staff, Board of Governors, etc., etc.

I can affirm without equivocation that the rate of medical errors resulting in severe injury or death is remarkably overstated and without validity. The Institute of Medicine has created a climate of fear that is devoid of validity.

I would urge Congress to avoid making the costs of healthcare even more unacceptable by introducing even more costly regulations.

Best wishes.

RICHARD E. CARLSON, M.D.

ECRI
PLYMOUTH MEETING, PENNSYLVANIA 19462–1298
September 11, 2002

The Honorable Phil English
Committee on Ways and Means
Pennsylvania—21st, Republican
1410 Longworth HOB
Washington, D.C. 20515–3821

Re: H.R. 4889: Patient Safety Improvement Act of 2002

Dear Congressman English:

On behalf of ECRI, I am writing to express our strong support for HR 4889, the "Patient Safety Improvement Act of 2002." As a Pennsylvania nonprofit patient safety organization with over thirty years of experience, ECRI commends your leadership in recognizing the critical need for redressing patient safety problems in our nation's healthcare system. ECRI runs a voluntary problem-reporting program (initiated in 1971), analyzes and investigates patient safety data, conducts evidenced-based systematic reviews, and disseminates risk reduction tools and information to healthcare providers. We work collaboratively with other organizations, hospitals, and providers on medication safety and other patient safety programs. Over the years, ECRI has been very successful in producing strides in patient safety—medical products, systems and practices have improved and injuries avoided. However, we remain all too aware of the longstanding barriers to problem reporting, and all too distressed when we see those problems repeat. Until healthcare providers are confident that their safety efforts will be used to help patients rather than hurt their own organizations, they will not divulge important information that can ultimately help to avoid another repeat performance.

We strongly recommend that the definition of a "patient safety organization" include organizations like ECRI, which has been collecting voluntary problem reports and safety data for over three decades. Our protocols mirror many of the ones outlined in the bill. We are an independent agency, we de-identify institutions, we disseminate safety information, and we provide feedback and assistance. We also have strict conflict-of-interest rules. We have worked very hard to maintain the trust and confidence of healthcare providers. The protections offered by the bill would promote even better reporting to ECRI, and better analysis and data as a result. The bill should recognize the importance of established safety organizations with a track record. Otherwise, it might thwart its own goals by inadvertently chilling the dissemination of data that is currently being shared on a voluntary basis.

ECRI provides highly regarded health technology assessment programs, issues numerous publications, and works on many government contracts—all of which bear on the safety and quality of healthcare. Our programs serve hospitals, long-term care facilities, government agencies, and payers across the nation as well as the public (see www.ecri.org for a more detailed description). We mention these other programs to emphasize that a patient safety organization may provide many programs and services. It is important that multifaceted activities should not preclude an organization from being designated as a "patient safety organization" under the Act. The current bill addresses this in Section 1181 (b) (2) by defining a patient safety organization as a private or public organization *or component thereof* that certifies that it conducts, as a primary activity, efforts to assist providers that report to such an organization. We urge you to retain this flexibility in the Act. It would be very distressing if an organization like ECRI, which has received thousands of patient safety reports and data from healthcare providers, were unable to be certified as a patient safety organization simply because its reporting program is one of many safety programs it operates. In fact, our interdisciplinary scope and breadth is an important factor in strengthening the quality of our work in patient safety.

ECRI is available to work with Congress to address improvements in patient safety and the matters addressed in HR 4889. Please feel free to contact me at (610) 825–6000 x5142 or Ronni P. Solomon, Esq. at (610)-825–6000 X5158.

Sincerely,

JEFFREY C. LERNER, PH.D.
President and Chief Executive Officer

Statement of the Society of Thoracic Surgeons

The Society of Thoracic Surgeons, representing essentially all board certified cardiac and thoracic surgeons in the United States, strongly urges the Congress to pass H.R. 4889, the Patient Safety Improvement Act of 2002.

This bill has been drafted following two years of careful study and numerous hearings on the ways in which Congress can best encourage hospitals, physicians, and other health care providers to collect and analyze adverse events and to share information on the means by which quality can continuously be improved. As the Institute of Medicine has emphasized, most weaknesses in health care are systemic and local; improvement requires the cooperation and participation of many individuals, and only through voluntary sharing of information is such systemic improvement possible at the local level.

H.R. 4889 will encourage the establishment of a voluntary national database, with confidentiality of reporting, that will permit the Department of Health and Human Services to analyze non-identifiable patient safety data. The bill will also encourage the analysis and sharing of this information at the local provider level. The Agency for Health Care Research and Quality should also be intimately involved in these data analyses.

The Society of Thoracic Surgeons established its voluntary National Cardiac Database (NCD) in 1989, and it has evolved into the type of analysis and feedback system for outcomes analysis that HR 4889 is proposing. The benefits of such a system, with analysis of data by objective professionals with the requisite medical and technical expertise, have been demonstrated by improvements in the care of cardiac surgery patients nationwide. Several state and regional cardiac surgical organizations, most notably the Northern New England Cardiovascular Disease Study Group have also demonstrated that, under conditions of confidentiality, information on best practices can readily be shared and analyzed within local and regional quality improvement organizations, with demonstrable improvements in medical practice.

The Society of Thoracic Surgeons' NCD for outcomes in cardiac surgery now includes over 1.8 million patient records. Currently, 529 institutions are submitting detailed data to the program. Through a partnership with the Duke Clinical Research Institute, database members are provided with site-specific risk-adjusted operative mortality, morbidity, and post-operative length of stay outcomes data. These feedback data permit the participating institutions to benchmark their own risk-adjusted—results against national and regional outcomes benchmarks and identify areas for process improvement.

In addition to the impetus provided for systemic quality improvement at participating institutions, the NCD enables qualified researchers to identify specific surgical techniques and processes of patient care that can improve outcomes following cardiac surgery.

A specific example of such a change is the increase in internal thoracic artery (ITA) use for primary CABG (Coronary Artery Bypass Grafting). In 1994, data from the STS NCD documented an overall increase in the use of ITA in the years 1989–1994; moreover, this study confirmed that ITA grafting was associated with a significant improvement in 30-day survival after CABG. Recently, a subsequent analysis from the NCD documented that even in elderly patients > age 75 years undergoing CABG, ITA grafting was strongly associated with decreased operative mortality (Ferguson, JTCVS, 2002). As a result of these and other studies, ITA use in CABG in the U.S. has increased steadily each year resulting in improved patient safety. This demonstrates the positive impact on outcomes that can—and has—resulted from a voluntary, confidential database. These data have been used in a national quality improvement randomized trial funded by the Agency for Healthcare Research and Quality (AHRQ) to the STS to promote the use of ITA grafting in the elderly, the results of which will be presented at the American Heart Association Meeting in November. Other STS led quality improvement efforts, most notably CQI efforts addressing the use of pre-operative beta-blockers to reduce mortality and morbidity following CABG, have been documented to improve CABG mortality (Ferguson, JAMA, 2002).

We believe that it is essential that health care data developed and reported for the purposes of quality improvement will remain confidential, and that this is true for this and other physician-led efforts in error identification and quality improvement. Within the STS database, this has been achieved through a sophisticated system of de-identifying data. It is equally essential that the data must be available locally, where it can be most effectively used by the providers to evaluate the processes of care, and that the data analyses, both local and national, be done by an objective 3rd party entity with the requisite medical and technical expertise to draw valid conclusions.

The STS as a medical specialty society with a documented track record in quality measurement and quality improvement believes that H.R. 4889 will encourage and facilitate greater exchange of needed patient safety and outcomes information throughout our nation's health care system. The combined professional ethic to "do the right thing" combined with such a NCD system has in part contributed to an almost 40% reduction in operative mortality nationwide for CABG between 1990–1999 in the US, despite an almost 40% increase in preoperative predicted surgical risk. We strongly support this proposed legislation and are proud that voluntary initiatives begun years ago by the Society of Thoracic Surgeons can now demonstrate that patient safety and outcomes reporting initiatives have directly and positively impacted on the safety and quality of CABG care nationwide.

○

APEX
TP
9780160707025
76901945—83